D1475647

THE
COMPLETE BOOK OF
KNIFE FIGHTING

THE
COMPLETE BOOK OF
KNIFE FIGHTING

The History of Knife Fighting Techniques
and Development of Fighting Knives,
Together With A

PRACTICAL METHOD
OF INSTRUCTION

by

WILLIAM L. CASSIDY

The Complete Book of Knife Fighting
Copyright (c) 1975
William L. Cassidy
All Rights Reserved.

Library of Congress Cat. No. 75-25207

ISBN: **0 87364 029 2**

PALADIN PRESS, Boulder, Colorado

PALADIN press

Post Office Box 1307
Boulder, Colorado 80302

This book is respectfully dedicated to the ''Soldiers of the Fortress of Faith,'' the *Ten Dzong Ma Mi* — known to the world as the N.V.D.A.

Also to Michel Peissel, author of *The Secret War in Tibet* — a book that is mightier than any sword.

This book is for those who only reluctantly take up arms; to fight not for causes, but for what is just.

TABLE OF CONTENTS

LIST OF ILLUSTRATIONS

PART III: THE TACTICS

WARNING

This book is for *information purposes only*. It is *not* a training manual. The techniques and drills depicted in this book are *extremely dangerous*. Do not attempt any of these techniques and drills without proper professional supervision and training. Attempting to do so can result in severe injury or death.

The author and the publisher expressly disclaim any liability from any damage or injuries that a user of this book may suffer. The author and the publisher expressly disclaim any liability from any damage or injuries to third parties from the user of this book.

PREFACE

Knives are remarkable instruments. They were, most certainly, among the first tools of man, and along the way they also evolved into his first weapon.

There is, indeed, a difference between a weapon and a tool, although the difference does not lie in the instrument itself.

The difference is of a finer stuff than mere iron or steel. It lies in the man who uses the instrument, the way he leads his life, and the choices that he makes.

Through the course of time, knives, their makers and their users have progressed more or less together. We have seen knives for survival, knives for decoration, knives for ceremony, knives for sport, and knives for conflict; depending upon the needs of the times and the disposition of the parties involved.

This is a book about knives for killing.

I can make no excuses for killing, as there are none. The practice of killing is a matter between a man and his conscience, his respect for life, and his own understanding of right and wrong.

I write this book with a heavy heart then, for in my own conscience I know the futility of its aims. To kill, and to keep on killing, is not only a means of destroying life, but a means of erasing whatever small good man has accomplished in his tenure on this planet. Yes, there is some small good in even the worst of men. This is something we must believe, if only to go on fighting for what we call freedom.

Yet if your purpose in reading this book is to perfect the art of killing, it will not be I who points an accusing finger, nor will I question the motives behind your decision. Instead, I will only ask you to remember.

Remember well a lesson men have continued to learn since time began, and which, it seems, each man must learn for himself. Remember that a moment of reckoning must surely come — whether that moment be as complex as the various judgements of man's laws, or as simple as life's last breath — and in that moment you will come to the same province as the beings you have killed: fish, fowl, mammal, or man. Your knife will be of no use to you then, nor your muscle, wit, or any other fleeting possession. The only thing left to you will be your deeds, the manner in which you walked upon the earth, the way you led your life and the choices you made.

This is not a sermon about the taking of life. This is just a brief appeal for reason and conscience. Were it not for troubled times, these words need never have been written.

William L. Cassidy
New York, New York
June, 1975

The author wishes to extend his appreciation to the following individuals, who have in some fashion contributed to the publication of this book: Alden Amos; Gene Tropp; Walter W. Collins; Peter J. Buxtun; W.D. Randall, Jr. and Gary Randall; Harold Hance; J. Phillip Langellier; Richard Merrill; David Waggott; William Russell; Clyde P. Peters; Sgt. Alfred K. Jayne, and Peder C. Lund, of Paladin Press. Very special thanks are also given to Dr. William Wennen — America's premier plastic surgeon.

The author would also like to acknowledge the very capable assistance of Robert W. Loveless and Raymond R. Randall — the two gentlemen who kindly consented to serve as models for the action photographs contained in this book. It would be difficult to find two men more qualified, or indeed, two better friends.

INTRODUCTION

Great are the legends and folklore which surround knife fighting. Greater still are the ill-conceived notions of its history, technique and tools. The book you have before you does not seek to add to either the legends or these misconceptions; rather, it seeks to clarify, digest and impartially — insofar as it is humanly possible to be impartial — portray what has become a remarkably confused practice.

The practice of which we speak is Western-style knife fighting; as distinct from Asian-style or any other differing form. It is a practice founded on the art of fence — a foundation solid or crumbling, depending on your point of view — and one which is, in our present day, enjoying substantial interest and enthusiasm from an ever-expanding number of practitioners.

In a private conversation with the author, noted American knifemaker W.D. Randall, Jr. said:

"I can see it all around me . . . something I really never expected to happen has happened. People from all walks of life are discarding the gun in favor of the knife. Many responsible persons — 'pillars of the society' you might say — have indicated to me that they now prefer the knife above all other weapons."

Mr. Randall's observations are, indeed, quite correct. With the increase of restrictive firearms legislation, as well as frequent incidents of senseless violence and lawlessness, men and women everywhere have begun to fall back on mankind's first weapon: the knife.

To serve this interest, albeit in a specialized fashion, the author has attempted to strip knife fighting to its bare bones; presenting this "Complete Book of Knife Fighting" in the form of three individual studies.

These studies we have termed *The Techniques; The Tools,* and *The Tactics.* With the first, we will examine the literature of knife fighting; compare the subtleties of the Western world's various techniques; learn more of the foundation upon which these techniques are based, and launch a brief, slightly evangelistic examination of the Eastern world's possible contributions.

In the second division of this book we will watch the pageant of weaponry. Beginning with a capsule history of fighting knife development, we will review major classes of design — noting both the good and bad features of each — and end with a bit of advice regarding knife concealment and methods of carry. All principal fighting knife designs or styles will be touched upon: from the justly famous dagger developed at the Commando Special Training Center in Achnacarry, Scotland by Fairbairn and Sykes, to the latest entry; the author's own *Tactical-Survivor,* developed for use in Latin America and the Middle East.

With this background and discussion behind us, we will begin the study of practical knife fighting. To the reader's possible dismay, this third division will not take the form of a course. If anything, our final area of study is a simple exposition of advice and logic. Methods are presented which the careful reader is invited to take or leave, according to his own abilities, motivations, and sense of reason. Any "pioneer" methods introduced in this section will be based upon the re-interpretation of existing knowledge, blended with techniques and attitudes introduced from the knife fighting systems of Asia.

With the exception of this Asian influence, the author has attempted to keep the present work on a straight and narrow path of Western-style *knife* fighting. For this reason, you will find but few words regarding bayonets, stick-fighting, or unarmed defense. The subject of bayonets was treated admirably by the British Small Arms School, which wrote in 1924:

"In the war the utility of the bayonet as a cutlass or dagger proved to be negligible, hence the demand for trench knives, clubs, etc. As a means of clearing brushwood, etc. it is one of the most futile instruments imaginable.

"As for killing shape it makes a very nasty wound, but is of bad section for penetration and worse for withdrawal."

The practices of stick-fighting and unarmed defense will, it is hoped, be better able to speak for themselves.

When first you read this book, you may find it a bit too philosophical for your taste. This is to be expected: knife fighting is not all glamor and glory, blood and guts. Respect for the practice of knife fighting breeds serious thought, and serious thought breeds better knife fighters. Understand this, and you will be well on your way to mastery of the art. Do not be disappointed with this emphasis on thought, nor, if you are truly serious about learning to use the knife, the absence of thrills and chills from these pages. Perfect physical activity begins with the mind, and in order to master the body, you must seek to first improve the body's master.

Beyond philosophy, however, we come to a small moment of truth: actual use of the knife for *killing*. Fine thoughts, comprehensive books, and custom-crafted fighting knives are fit companions in the safety of home or barracks. In the field of conflict it is only man himself who can make final judgement.

This book is a prelude and a preparation: a spring-board for further research and greater study. Take what you read here, examine it well, and subject it to your own set of tests. Practice what you will learn from these pages, or the pages of the other books here recommended. Practice seriously, *before* your own moment of truth. Think deeply *before* your own final judgement.

To preserve your own life, the life of a loved one, or to further a goal you believe is just, it is sometimes necessary to take the life of another. This book, nor any other book cannot teach you to do this. Books may only tell you what might happen, but never what will.

Note: In the following work, instructions or descriptions have been written as though all parties involved were right-handed. In virtually all cases herein, left-handed persons should merely read these instructions or descriptions as if the reverse had been written. Where this is not the case, appropriate commentaries have been appended.

With only minor exceptions, this work has been written in the masculine gender. This is not meant to imply that women are not well-suited to knife fighting, or are in any way inferior. It is only a convenience of the author.

PART I: THE TECHNIQUES

HISTORICAL DEVELOPMENT

To the student of the sword, or rapier, the responsibility of scholarship is easily served by a visit to any well-selected library. There he will find endless references to books, tracts and monographs treating every facet of his combative discipline. He may, if he so requires, study his art in any of a dozen languages, and with very little effort, should be able to compile a bibliography of these works tracing back to the 14th century.

The student of knife fighting, as a specialized technique, is not so fortunate. The written history of knife fighting is somewhat more select and confined; being largely a collection of small booklets and pamphlets, leaflets and half-finished manuscripts. Although the practice of conflict with edged weapons encompasses virtually all countries and civilizations, as far as the written word is concerned, knife fighting has played but a small role.

The reason for this disparity of information may be found by discovering the level of esteem to which knife fighting was held in earliest record. In *Trattato di Scienza d'Arme,* published in 1604, M. Camillo Agrippa, the great fencing theorist, makes mention of the dagger only as a supplement to the rapier. Later writers were less kindly disposed, declaring the dagger or knife ''suitable only for sticking frogs,'' and thus wholly distasteful to the better class of men.

In the days when sword and rapier held sway, knife fighting was the realm of peasants and vagabonds. Gentlemen of breeding utilized the dagger or knife only as a matter of convenience, or as a parrying weapon in connection with the sword.

By the 18th and 19th centuries, however, the sword was rapidly falling before the knife. It is in this time period that we begin to see the advent of published works upon the particular subject of knife fighting. *Manual del Baratero ō Arte de Manejar la Navaja el Cuchillo y la Tijera de los Jitanos,* published in Madrid, in 1849, is an oft-cited example. This work deals with the techniques of knife and scissor fighting as practiced by Spanish gypsies.

In 19th century America, schools of knife fighting were established, inspired by the widely published exploits of James Bowie. These schools, many of which were situated in or around New Orleans, purported to teach the art and science of Bowie knife and "Arkansas Toothpick" handling. They began, for the most part, in the late 1820's and early 1830's, and apparently enjoyed a substantial following until restrictive legislation forced their demise.

The introduction of the revolver caused the practice of knife fighting to retreat from favor, and few published references (other than the purely anecdotal), can be found from the period of about 1860 to the early 1900's.

With the beginning of World War I, interest in knife fighting once again ascended to general popularity. In America, a great deal of thought and discussion was devoted to equipment and combat techniques for trench warfare. Naturally, this led to renewed interest in the knife.

At the close of World War I, interest in knife fighting briefly subsided, to be kept alive by individuals rather than nations. On the eve of World War II, however, the practice of knife fighting was beginning upon what could rightfully be called its renaissance period.

THE RENAISSANCE
OF KNIFE FIGHTING

World War II saw the practice of knife fighting become formalized into two basic schools of methodology, each having certain refinements of technique in common with the other. In addition, the war years also produced a flurry of knife fighting pamphlets and texts, as never before witnessed in the history of the art.

The two schools mentioned above enjoyed their greatest development during the decade of 1940-1950. Their creation was the result of effort put forth by four dedicated edged weapons theorists: Major W.E. Fairbairn, Lieutenant-Colonel A.J.D. Biddle,

Lieutenant-Colonel Rex Applegate, and former U.S. Marine John Styers.

To Major Fairbairn, we owe the so-called *Commando Technique,* with extensive later refinements provided by Lieutenant-Colonel Applegate. This technique, known to some as the ''Shanghai School,'' (After the city where Major Fairbairn first developed his theories), was widely favored by British Commandos, O.S.S. operatives, and the First Special Service Force. It has since formed the basis for instruction given to all members of the United States Armed Forces.

The second school of practice, variously referred to as the *Sabre Technique,* or ''Formal School,'' was developed by Lieutenant-Colonel Biddle, and was once adopted as the official method of training the U.S. Marine Corps. This school saw its greatest refinement at the hands of John Styers, and his collaborator, Karl Schuon. Styers became quite a proselyte of Biddle's methods (later termed the ''Styers Method''); touring various Marine, Army and Air Force bases around the United States, conducting special courses. The Styers Method has, as a result, became quite a favorite with many U.S. troops, and is reputed to be the method by which this country's clandestine operatives are instructed.

We will here begin an individual study of these men and their works. The author has chosen Fairbairn, Biddle, Applegate and Styers as a focal point, not only because of their immense contributions to the art of knife fighting, but their published works as well. By virtue of these published works, they are the instructors most familiar to the average student of knife fighting. We will discuss them here in the relative order of their appearance.

W.E. Fairbairn

Perhaps no one man has more influenced the art and science of close-quarter combat technique than Major W.E. Fairbairn: Assistant Commissioner (from 1927 to 1940), of the Shanghai Municipal Police; author of an approved standard Individual Combat instruction for the British Army, and, with E.A. Sykes, designer of the now legendary Fairbairn-Sykes Fighting Knife.

Beginning in 1942, with the publication of his book *Get Tough! How to Win in Hand-to-Hand Fighting,* (published in England as *All-In Fighting),* Fairbairn's gospel has since spread to virtually every military and police force on the face of the globe, and has certainly influenced such authorities as Biddle, Applegate, Styers, and others...

This, in itself, is rather surprising, for *Get Tough!* devotes but little text to the subject of knife fighting. Presumably, Fairbairn's

Figure 1

Title page to *Trattato di Scienza d'Arme*, published in 1604, showing portrait of Agrippa, the great fencing theorist.

Figure 2

The dagger as adjunct to rapier, according to Agrippa.

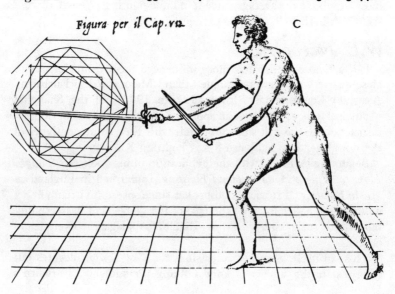

main influence came from the scores of young men he personally trained in the use of the knife.

What *Get Tough!* did accomplish, however, was the isolation and identification of the principal body areas most vulnerable to knife attack, and the introduction of structure and thought to what had formerly been the province of street-brawlers.

To Fairbairn's logical way of thinking, in order to begin upon the study of knife fighting, it was first necessary to learn the vital areas of a man's body, and then proceed to build a system of reaching them. All else was discarded as unnecessary.

Although there are many nerve ganglia, blood vessels and ligaments in reach of the ordinary knife blade; from a tactical standpoint, Fairbairn advocated but six target areas, as follows:

1. Brachial Artery
2. Radial Artery
3. Carotid Artery
4. Subclavian Artery
5. Heart
6. Stomach

These six areas, he felt, were the areas most accessible to the knife fighter: the areas which, when cut or stabbed with full force, would be most likely to cause death, and the areas which, when cut or stabbed with but moderate force would still create the greatest shock.

Fairbairn then carried his research a bit further, and through some unknown agency, produced a detailed "Timetable of Death." A cut or thrust to each respective area was evaluated in terms of the vulnerable point's depth below the surface of the epidermis, time elapsed until loss of consciousness, and time elapsed until death. Whether Fairbairn's findings were purely theoretical, being taken from some medical text, or whether they were the result of more practical research is a matter for conjecture.

According to Fairbairn's timetable, we are able to surmise that strikes to the Carotid Artery, Subclavian Artery, and Heart are the most effective, while those to the Radial Artery, Brachial Artery, and Stomach are the least effective, if only in more or less relative terms. Nevertheless, Fairbairn did advocate cuts and slashes to the Radial, Brachial and Stomach areas, presumably for their shock value. As to the Subclavian Artery, Fairbairn gave this sage advice:

"This is not an easy artery to cut with a knife, but, once cut, your opponent will drop, and no tourniquet or any help of man can save him."

Indeed, many latter-day practitioners of knife fighting have all but discarded the Subclavian cut, as it requires the knife to be held in a less than satisfactory grip.

As mentioned previously, Major Fairbairn was employed as Assistant Commissioner of the Shanghai Municipal Police from 1927 to 1940. During this period he necessarily came in contact with a great many members of the U.S. Marine Corps, stationed in China in large numbers from about 1927 to 1940. These were the men who would later be responsible for the enormous spread of Fairbairn's combat methods.

W.E. Fairbairn's "Timetable of Death," from his book *Get Tough!* This picture also illustrates the approximate location of vital target areas. (Used Here by Permission).

Figure 3

No.	Name of Artery	Size	Depth below Surface in inches	Loss of Consciousness in seconds	Death	
1....	Brachial	Medium	½	14	1½	Min.
2....	Radial	Small	¼	30	2	"
3....	Carotid	Large	1½	5	12	Sec.
4....	Subclavian	Large	2½	2	3½	"
5....	(Heart)	—	3½	Instantaneous	3	"
6....	(Stomach)	—	5	Depending on depth of cut		

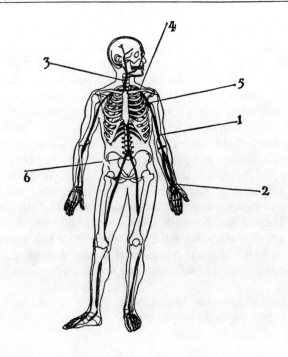

Beginning in the early 1930's, Major Fairbairn took the opportunity to become acquainted with a number of the officers in his jurisdiction; infecting them with his enthusiasm for the novel method of close-quarter combat he termed "Defendu." Defendu was, actually, a highly westernized version of *Jiu-Jitsu.*

One officer so infected was 1st Lieutenant Samuel G. Taxis. Lieutenant Taxis was Battalion Instructor to the 4th Marines, and trainer of the Marine Boxing Team which won the Boxing Championship of China. More importantly, he was also a former pupil of Lieutenant-Colonel A.J.D. Biddle; having received his first instruction from Biddle while the latter was Individual Combat Instructor at the U.S.M.C. Basic School for Officers.

Discovering their common interests, Fairbairn and Taxis undertook to instruct large numbers of the 4th Marines in both Defendu and knife fighting. In at least one instance, it is recorded that Fairbairn and Taxis offered this instruction to an armed contingent of 200 Sikh police, then stationed in Shanghai. It would seem from this that Fairbairn's methods knew no international boundaries.

Lieutenant Taxis returned to the United States about 1935-'36, heavily steeped in Fairbairn's methods. Upon his arrival, Taxis was able to inform his old instructor, Biddle, of the Fairbairn innovations. Suitably impressed, Biddle decided to incorporate many of these methods into his famous book, *Do or Die.* Thus, to 1st Lieutenant Samuel G. Taxis, by way of Lieutenant-Colonel Biddle, we owe the introduction of Major W.E. Fairbairns' methods to the United States.

A.J.D. Biddle

Lieutenant-Colonel A.J. Drexel Biddle, U.S.M.C.R. was the classicist of knife fighting, its grandest gentleman and finest scholar. He is the recognized dean of American close quarter combat instruction, and holder of knife fighting's most impressive credentials.

Biddle began his instruction in knife, sword, and bayonet under Major William J. Herrmann, an early American Fencing Champion and World's Bayonet Fighting Champion. Later, he was to receive instruction from Britain's J.H. Hawkins, sword instructor of the King's Royal Horse Guards. Other instructors with whom Biddle studied extensively were Broadsword Champion M. Thomas, International Sword Champion Jean-Marie Surget, and fencing master J. Martinez Castello, of New York.

During the early 1930's, Biddle served as Individual Combat Instructor of the U.S.M.C. Basic School for Officers, and as Professor on the Faculty of the Federal Bureau of Investigation, U.S. Department of Justice.

In 1935, Biddle was invited to become Individual Combat Instructor of the Fifth Regiment, U.S.M.C., stationed in Quantico. While so engaged, and at the suggestion of his commanding officer, Biddle began work on his justly famous book, *Do or Die: A Supplementary Manual on Individual Combat.*

Published in 1937, *Do or Die* was the culminating effort of over twenty years spent observing, studying and practicing the various arts of self-defense. As a tribute to Biddle's work, *Do or Die* bears the following citation on its title page:

"This manual has been accepted by the United States Marine Corps and issued as a guide for training in 'Individual Combat.' "

By virtue of his extensive training in broadsword and *epee*, Biddle felt that classic swordsmanship would form an excellent basis for improved knife fighting instruction. His belief in the need for such improvement is underscored by these introductory lines from Part II of *Do and Die,* the chapter on knife fighting:

"Considerable space in this treatise is given to knife fighting, because the Marines serve in many knife fighting countries and are frequently called upon to capture or fight against the dagger, machete or bolo "

So strong was Biddle's indoctrination into the use of the sword, that his entire method of instruction is built upon such maneuvers as *In-quartata, Passata Sotto,* and other, similar movements well-known to the duellist. In spite of his introductory remarks, nowhere does Biddle acknowledge the fact that the users of ''dagger, machete or bolo'' may not have been gentlemen, well-schooled in the tenets of swordsmanship and fair play.

This was Biddle's greatest weakness. He was a gentleman instructing other gentlemen in the *ritual* of knife fighting. As such, many of the methods he advocated come down to us as nothing more than quaint reminders of an earlier (and perhaps better), age of conflict.

Biddle's methods did, however, make a singularly valuable contribution to the formalized instruction of knife fighting: the hand-cut. The hand-cut is described in his own words:

"The hand-cut is particularly prescribed for use with the bayonet as knife and is an exquisitely scientific movement, taken from the sword and known to few others than scienced swordsmen."

For the first time in recent history, the knife fighter was being counseled not to strike full to the heart, throat, or other killing area, but to instead concentrate his efforts upon the hand and arm of his adversary. In this fashion it was felt that the knife fighter would gain the greatest advantage over the unskilled — although presumably

Figure 4

In-quartata, according to A.J.D. Biddle, as illustrated in his book *Do or Die*. This picture serves to strengthen the impression that Biddle's movements were somewhat out-moded by the 1940's. (Used Here by Permission).

Dagger fighting in the 16th century.   **Figure 5**

armed — opponent. Biddle acknowledged, and wisely, that it is not always possible to make the first blow the last.

Biddle advocated the hand-cut as the principal method of neutralizing what he termed the "underhand or overhand dagger fighter." Here, he refers to the two common methods of grasping a knife or dagger, which in later times we have come to term the Ice-Pick and Hammer Grip (see Part III: Tactics). As certain of the accompanying illustrations will show, underhand and overhand dagger fighting was well established in history; the practice being encouraged by early-day knife fighting instructors.

Well into his chapter on knife fighting, Biddle abruptly changes course from the classic to the more mundane. In doing so, he makes these surprising statements:

". . . The following course of instruction teaches the use of the knife as prescribed by the late Colonel James Bowie, U.S.A."

". . . The following course of instruction is after the teachings of the Bowie knife as prescribed by the Colonel himself: he was a celebrated sword duellist."

Underhand guard position of the 16th century.   Figure 6

Overhand dagger fighting of the 17th century.   **Figure 7**

These remarks are followed by other, equally ficticious inventions. As Bowie scholars and historians will readily tell you, there is no evidence whatsoever to indicate that —

1. Bowie ever gave "instruction" in the use of the Bowie knife;
2. Bowie was ever considered a "celebrated sword duellist."

Eye-witness accounts published contemporaneous with Bowie's most famous "duel" — the rough-and-tumble Vidalia Sandbar Fight — show that the event was more of a brawl than anything else, and Bowie certainly carried no sword. Nowhere, in fact, in Bowie's history is there any report that he even *owned* a sword. As to his supposed instruction: history tells us that Bowie was far too occupied with land-swindling, slave-running and other mercenary activities to even consider conducting classes in knife fighting.

Biddle's grasp of James Bowie's influence on knife fighting was wholly incorrect. One supposes he included the above remarks in an attempt to indoctrinate the reader into believing he was carrying on a fine tradition of American knife fighting.

In his book, Biddle illustrated but seven basic moves. We will examine these moves more fully in Part III: Tactics, and include them here only to quickly familiarize the reader with Biddle's principal contributions.

These seven moves are as follows:

1. The Guard Position
2. Outside Parry and Grab
3. Inside Parry and Grab
4. *In-quartata*
5. *Stoccata*
6. *Passata Sotto*
7. Defense against overhand attack

In addition, counsel was given on the important aspects of blade position, foot-work, and arm placement. This matter of arm placement, or use of the free hand, was a significant development in its day.

Briefly, the knife fighter was advised to use his knife much in the manner of a rapier; executing rapier-like thrusts with the knife hand, while the free arm was thrown straight to the rear. This was thought to add velocity and balance to the maneuver. Although this is a classic movement of sword-play, it is not out of place in modern knife fighting.

In summary, we may say that while not a definitive method of knife fighting, Biddle's techniques were a first attempt at formalizing the practice of knife fighting into an art which could be taught, rather than acquired. We also credit him with the westernization of knife fighting, due to his application of sword and rapier technique as taught by the great French, Italian and English fencing masters.

Biddle's works did leave a sizeable vacuum, however, and were all but discarded by the 1940's. During this critical period in our nation's history, another, more practical theorist was to make his appearance.

Rex Applegate

If we are to characterize Fairbairn as the most influential man in close-quarter combat technique, and Biddle as its classicist, then we must certainly characterize Lieutenant-Colonel Rex Applegate as the most influential man in close-quarter knife fighting. Applegate is the scientist of knife fighting; its deepest thinker, and best known strategist.

Applegate's famous book, *Kill or Get Killed,* originally published c July, 1943 by the Military Service Publishing Company, provided the first really in-depth treatment of the subject of knife fighting ever published in the United States. As a measure of this book's

Figure 8

The legendary Rex Applegate, America's most practical knife fighting instructor, shown here demonstrating the Fence Grip. (reprinted from *Kill or Get Killed,* Copyright (C) 1961 The Stackpole Company, Used Here by Permission).

popularity, it might be well to here mention that it has gone through four editions and seven printings. This same material, in a substantially identical form, was later published in Applegate's *Crowd and Riot Control;* John and Robert Ek's *Your Silent Partner,* and *The Fighting Knife,* by W.D. Randall, Jr., creator of the well-known Randall-Made knives.

What Applegate accomplished, more than any other writer before or since, was the systematic exposition of knife fighting in its many and varied forms. He covered the art in great detail, throwing light on such arcane areas as methods of attack; sentry killing; concealment; parry defenses; block defenses; racial preferences, and, more importantly, the over-all psychology of the art.

From Applegate we learn of such niceties as the slash attack, backhand assassination techniques, and wrist holsters. All the sort of stuff that the more romantic notions of knife fighting feed upon, portrayed in a decidedly unromantic, no-nonsense fashion. When it comes to knife fighting, Applegate is a practical man, and this practicality shows throughout all of his writings on the subject.

If we generalize Lieutenant-Colonel Applegate's contributions to knife fighting, it will have to be in terms of this practicality. Applegate *systemitized* knife fighting, providing the student with a means to quickly attain proficiency, through an understanding of knife fighting's various problems.

Applegate began by assigning categories to knife wielders, as follows:

1. The Trained Fighter
2. The Unskilled Fighter
3. The Slasher

Next, he proceeded to instruct the student in the best means of either attacking or defending against each. Applegate was, however, by no means naive enough to believe that all knife wielders could be groupd into convenient categories. Under the heading *Unskilled Attack,* Applegate had this to say:

"A knowledge of defense against knife attacks of this kind is necessary, but it is a serious omission by any instructor to place all knife users in this category and to conduct a training program accordingly."

In our modern day, Applegate's words may sound like an understatement of acknowledged fact. A glance at many current training programs will, however, underscore the urgency of Colonel Applegate's words.

Applegate also provided the first true exposition of the *Parry Defense.* Where Fairbairn (and others) relied upon blocking techniques for unarmed defense against the knife, Applegate saw the potential danger in attempting to block unusually strong or fanatical individuals. Perhaps more than anything else, Applegate wanted his techniques to rely more upon cunning and deft handling than brute force.

Figure 9

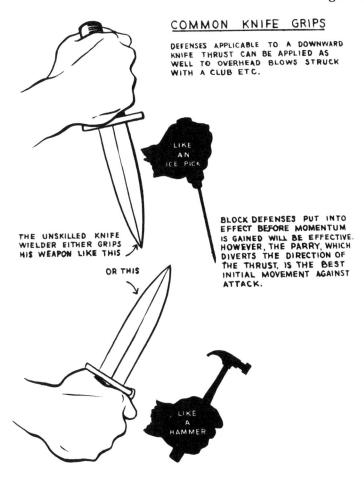

COMMON KNIFE GRIPS

DEFENSES APPLICABLE TO A DOWNWARD KNIFE THRUST CAN BE APPLIED AS WELL TO OVERHEAD BLOWS STRUCK WITH A CLUB ETC.

LIKE AN ICE PICK

BLOCK DEFENSES PUT INTO EFFECT BEFORE MOMENTUM IS GAINED WILL BE EFFECTIVE. HOWEVER, THE PARRY, WHICH DIVERTS THE DIRECTION OF THE THRUST, IS THE BEST INITIAL MOVEMENT AGAINST ATTACK.

THE UNSKILLED KNIFE WIELDER EITHER GRIPS HIS WEAPON LIKE THIS

OR THIS

LIKE A HAMMER

Common knife grips acknowledged by Applegate. (reprinted from *Kill or Get Killed*, Copyright (C) 1961 The Stackpole Company, Used Here by Permission).

Figure 10

The great John Styers, here demonstrating perfect guard position. A large measure of credit is due Styers for his excellent work with the military. (reprinted from *Cold Steel*, Used Here by Permission).

John Styers

Through Fairbairn we arrived at Applegate. Through Biddle, we arrive at former Marine John Styers: the fourth member of America's great quartet of knife fighting experts.

It is evident that Styers was a star pupil of the late Lieutenant-Colonel Biddle, for the former's now-famous book *Cold Steel,* is liberally infused with the latter's theories. There are, however, but few of the quaint archaisms proposed by Biddle, for like Rex Applegate, John Styers seems to be an eminently practical man.

Briefly, Styers divided his course of instruction into five major, and nine minor categories. An outline of his technique would look like this:

      I. Grip
     II. Stance
        1. The Sabre Stance
        2. The Knife Duellist Stance
   III. The Thrust
   IV. The Cut
        1. The Vertical Cut
        2. The Horizontal Cut
        3. The Hand Cut
    V. Technique
        1. Distance (between opponents)
        2. Targets
        3. *In-quartata*
        4. *Passata Sotto*

When we examine this outline, we of course realize the extent to which Styers was influenced by Biddle, due to the emphasis placed on sword technique. Basically, Styers' work may be thought of as an extension, or amplification of Biddle's work in this area.

What Styers attempted to do, however, was to integrate this sword technique into the practice of knife fighting somewhat more fully; modifying it (where necessary), to allow for the technical peculiarities of the weapon he advocated: the Bowie knife.

For this reason, Styers devotes considerable space to what he calls the "natural whipping action" of the knife, observing that this momentum of the blade may be used to greatest advantage when making the vertical, or hand cuts. In this case, "whip action" is defined as the Bowie knife's natural inclination to bob up and down (somewhat like a diving board), when extended in a full-length, abruptly terminated thrust.

Styers continues, to give valuable insight to the physical relationship between muscle and steel. This relationship may be thought of in terms of the natural, physical *tensions* which develop when the weapon is used. To illustrate, Styers offers the following advice:

"*. . . The blade must avoid making circles at the full extension of the arm. These circles are the result of forced action of the wrist or forearm, preventing the natural action of the blade.*"

This obviously is the statement of a man greatly in harmony with his weapon, and bespeaks a painstaking examination of knife use. To further illustrate, consider Styers' advice regarding proper grip, stated briefly and clearly:

"*1. Keep the wrist locked at all times; 2. Don't arch the thumb on the thumb guard; 3. Keep the blade on line with the forearm.*"

Again, this advice is based on Styers' observations of the relationship between man and knife. This, the author believes, is Styers' principal contribution to the art of knife fighting. To him we owe the introduction of *weapon consciousness*, something which — while not altogether lacking from previous methods — was nevertheless glossed over.

Styers has placed his greatest emphasis on agility and maneuverability. Quickness and deft handling are, to him, the qualities most highly prized in modern knife fighting. With this we must agree. Whether this agility and deftness should be based upon the European system of sword science, is a question we will take up in the succeeding paragraphs.

THE RATIONALE OF TECHNIQUE

Up until this point, we have been concerned with a discussion of knife fighting as it is *taught in America today.* Now we will examine the base upon which these methods of instruction have been founded. At the same time, we will launch an investigation into the great edged weapons systems of the East, particularly those of Japan.

"*In the history of the dagger and its use in combat, we can see many of the principles governing the development and use of the sword.*"

So writes Arthur Wise, in his excellent book *The Art and History of Personal Combat.* It is an accurate statement, for it seems that much of what we know about the techniques of knife fighting has come to us through the many and varied practices of swordsmanship. We may further qualify this statement by adding that the principles in questions are large European, or Western in origin.

Egerton Castle, writing in *Schools and Masters of Fence: From the Middle Ages to the End of the Eighteenth Century* (London, 1892), makes the following statement:

Figure 11

These two worthies illustrate what is meant by "closing in and wrestling," as practiced in 16th century Germany.

"The dagger has been at most times, and in all countries, the natural companion of the sword, and for obvious reasons: a reversion to 'natural fighting,' by closing in and wrestling, was always a likely termination to a more civilized and scientific combat."

The clue here, as we shall soon see, is the word "civilized." Knife or dagger fighting, as pointed out earlier, was never very highly regarded among early edged weapons systems. How then did knife fighting come to be governed by the principles of swordsmanship? To answer this question, and to illustrate the "westernization" of knife fighting, it is necessary for us to briefly return to the period of the sword's decline.

Many scholars trace the decline of the sword to the abolishment of *Compagnie des Maitres en fait d'Arme des Acadmies du Roi en la Ville et Faubourg de Paris,* (the supreme authority on matters of sword science), during the French Revolution. The Revolution spelled the doom not only of the leisured class of gentlemen, many of them devoted *habitues* of the French Academy, but of the "gentleman's weapon," the sword.

Prior to the Revolution, a great and vast system of sword use had covered the whole of Europe. Sword use had become more of a sport than a means of combat, with fencing taking on all the characteristics of a parlour diversion. Each country boasted their national hero, their Sword Academy, and each locality their favored instructor. Duels were fought purely for the knowing of which school or technique was

Figure 12

Coat of Arms granted to the French Academy in 1656 by Louis XIV. (Author's collection)

"better" and for no other reason. Thus, we can see where sharp distinctions were made between mere conflicts, and conflicts where honor, or skill were involved. This is the notion of "civilized" sword use mentioned earlier.

After the Revolution, with the great French Academy in disarray, similar traditions, such as those of the Spanish and Italian sword masters, soon ceased to exist. Public focus shifted to weapons a bit more practical, or military in nature.

Naturally, the dagger and knife, being weapons of the populace, received wide favor in the Socialistic climate of post-Revolution Europe. As with most Socialistic endeavors, however, one badge of rank was removed merely to be replaced by another. The dagger, knife, or *stiletto,* once the weapons of vagabonds, and, perversely, gentlemen, again became *de rigueur.* As before, methods of instruction were erected around their use.

In searching for appropriate methods of instruction, those who favored the knife were forced to return to the sword sciences of pre-Revolution days! The logic here demanded that if the knife were, indeed, an edged weapon, it behooved the knife fighter to base his art upon the maneuvers of the Queen of Edged Weapons: the sword. Thus, the cycle of edged weapons instruction was complete, after much sound and fury which, in the end, signified really nothing.

THE EASTERN SCIENCE

As we have seen, each of the four great instructors, Fairbairn, Biddle, Applegate and Styers, were men well-schooled in the art of fence. Because of this schooling, and because of the influence each brought to the other, it is extremely difficult for us to separate their techniques from the rich fabric of European swordsmanship.

With the possible exception of Fairbairn, it is doubtful that any of these men were ever exposed to the purely Eastern or Oriental methods of blade-handling.In Fairbairn's case it may be supposed that like all good Colonialists, what little exposure he might have had was quickly passed over as imperfect. Witness, for example, the Oriental art of *jiu-jitsu* quickly becoming ''Defendu'' at his hands.

Be this as it may, it is the author's belief that the Oriental science of blade use is far superior to the European, and the art of knife fighting would receive much benefit from a careful investigation of the Oriental techniques. Accordingly, we will here include the brief exposition of a few specifics gleaned from the Japanese. Why Japan you ask? Why not India, Persia, Arabia or China? We choose Japan for the simple reason that history has shown us well the Japanese Samurai were the greatest masters of live steel who ever lived.

Iai-jutsu and Kenjutsu

The two major disciplines whereby Samurai were instructed in the use of edged weapons are known as *Iai-jutsu* and *Kenjutsu.* Iai-jutsu is the study of drawing the sword, while Kenjutsu is the study of actual conflict. Both of these disciplines, if properly utilized, bring an entirely new dimension to our primarily westernized practice of knife fighting.

The Japanese hold a number of concepts which should be regarded as extremely important by the modern knife fighter. These concepts are as follows:

1. Combative-engagement distance *(ma-ai)*
2. Opportunity *(suki)*
3. Domination *(zanshin)*
4. Continuity of Action

To the above we will add a fifth concept: that of *kobo-ichi,* defined by the great martial arts scholar Donn F. Draeger as ''the phenomena by which offensive and defensive actions are basically one.'' As we will see, all these concepts act together, forming a larger, cohesive whole.

Combat-engagement distance is the distance from one another at which two opponents will clash. In its elemental sense, it is a concept which has been acknowledged by all swordsmen and knife fighters. In our present day, we see it presented by John Styers, under the relative heading "Distance."

It is not, however, a predetermined distance, nor, ideally, should it be measured in feet or inches. Combat distance is a *mental attitude* of the man in harmony with his own forces: forces like fear, decision-making, emotional response and aggression.

In a gross physical sense, combat distance is supposed to be determined by the particular weapon one is facing. Spiritually, however, the author believes it is the spontaneous unleashing of *will* upon reaching the correct crescendo of all emotional and physical focus. In this sense, combat distance would involve the seizure of opportunity *(suki),* although it is the author's belief that this seizure should not involve the decision-making process.

In any given conflict, one's goal should be that of gaining maximum advantage through every physical and mental action. This goal may be achieved in one of two ways —

1. Immediately establishing superiority over the situation;

2. Allowing each and every mental and physical action to build upon the other, until a climax is reached and the adversary falls.

Inherent in this last is the idea of all defensive and offensive actions being principally the same thing. Obviously, if you are to gain maximum advantage or superiority, your every action must be perfect and blameless. Every motion must defend you, weaken your opponent's defense, and establish your domination, *all at the same time.*

Here too, we may see what is meant by *continuity of action.* This is not a purely Japanese concept, but is well established in the causual sciences of all Asia. Briefly, and very basically, we can illustrate this concept by using the example of a hypothetical knife fight:

In our imaginary fight, one adversary directs a thrust to the other adversary's throat. To our western way of thinking, this single thrust would constitute but a single activity, *complete in itself.* You will notice that all of the methods previously discussed, whether authored by Fairbairn, Biddle, Applegate or Styers, gave primary emphasis to such singular actions, and each action was treated separately, as a thing apart from the total conflict.

Continuity, on the other hand, demands that the thrust be considered as merely one small element of a larger action —

1. The fight itself;

2. The opportunity to direct thrusts;

3. The thrusts themselves;

4. The return to battery position.

Each element acts upon the other, but they do not act independently. Quite the contrary: the above four elements are taken *collectively,* and thus represent the whole of the fight.

One can easily see that knife fighting is somewhat like playing pocket billiards: it is only possible to "run the table" (or kill one's opponent), if one correctly sets up each successive "shot" (the strike or thrust), through the use of proper "english" (the awareness of continuity of action). Any movement on the part of the figher must immediately place him in a position where —

1. He is not open to counter-attack;
2. He is firmly grounded to continue the conflict.

For this process to be achieved spontaneously, or without formal, concentrated mental effort, obviously requires a great deal of training in the more practical aspects of conflict. In essence, the ability to "act without thinking," is best gained through actual, mortal combat.

To many of us, the opportunities for actual engagement are slight, and this is really as it should be. To achieve the purpose at hand then, it has been necessary to devise methods by which this experience may be gained, without the necessity of bloodshed. The Japanese call their particular method *sotai renshu:* the development of the habit of resourcefulness in combat through training against a partner. As any student of the marital arts will recognize, this is a method built upon the practice of the "pulled punch." Here we are not dealing with bare fists, however, but the prospect of live steel, which is an ideal way to quicken anyone's wits.

The practice of *sotai renshu* is very formal, and involves a great deal of prior training. As such, it would be a mistake for us to here consider the specifics of how it is done. We may, however, quickly outline a method by which the interested knife fighter may gain many of the benefits of *sotai renshu.*

To practice this method, which we will call sparring, it is necessary to have wooden practice knives, and a suitable partner. A large bed-sheet is also needed, and a well-lighted, properly ventilated area to work in. It should be noted that the wooden practice knives must closely approximate the size and weight of the knives which would be used in actual combat. This may be accomplished by duplicating the combat knife in wood, and then filling the blade and handle with lead as needed.

First, the bed-sheet is laid smooth upon the ground, and each sparring partner takes up his position at either edge. Next, the knife arm is extended full length, from the shoulder, at right angles to the body. With the knife in the hand, the distance to which the arm is extended is noted, and a semi-circle is drawn upon the bed sheet, with the feet being used as the pivotal point. (See illustration). This process is repeated for each partner, and the purpose of it is to graphically represent the *effective field of action* each player enjoys.

Figure 13

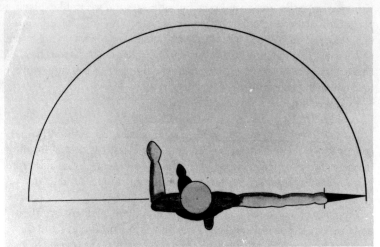

**Effective Field of Action is, in essence, nothing more than "reach."
Proper awareness of EFA is crucial, however, and should be developed.**

At this point, the preliminaries are over, and it is time to begin actual practice. Each partner is resolved to strike as many telling blows on the other as he possibly can: at the same time taking care not to be struck himself. The partners take up their positions, and at a pre-arranged signal —

1. Knives are drawn;
2. Stance is taken;
3. Engagement is made;
4. Return to battery position is made.

Briefly, the process works something like this: You are faced with a situation requiring engagement. You face your opponent, draw your weapon, strike him, and return to battery (correct stance), *all in one continuous motion.* Your opponent attempts to retaliate, but you are, to him, seemingly always in the most defensible position. Your strikes should not be merely one-point strikes to a particular target. Instead, you should seek to inflict maximum damage at the time when you are most vulnerable — *when you are inside your partner's field of action.*

Thus sparring strikes should be made with force, and with the intention of letting your opponent know he's been hit. Partners are warned not to take turns being the "aggressor," or "defender," as in a knife fight, *both parties are the aggressor!* The only sacrifice made to form in the early stages of this sparring is that after every engagement, both partners *must* return to battery position. After practice has progressed to the point where both partners are confident of their abilities, this rule is broken, and action continues for timed intervals of three to five minutes, five such intervals making a bout.

The quick return to battery after engagement has the following beneficial qualities —

1. The partners are better able to count the number of blows each has landed;

2. The partners are constantly developing the notion of continuity, and cultivating awareness.

It should be mentioned here that the above is merely one method of knife training, and several other methods are available to the interested student. These may be found by studying the various Field Manuals of the Armed Forces, or from the martial arts academies.

PART II: THE TOOLS

HISTORICAL DEVELOPMENT

In 1966, Harold L. Peterson wrote his now well known book, *Daggers & Fighting Knives of the Western World,* which almost immediately gained a wide following among U.S. and British edged weapons enthusiasts. Many of the popular beliefs regarding the development of the dagger and fighting knife may be traced directly to this book, and rightfully so, for it is among the finest ever written on the subject.

According to Peterson, although copper knives and daggers were being made in Egypt, Mesopotamia, and other areas of the Near East by about 6500 B.C., the true fighting knife did not appear until approximately 4500-3500 B.C. It is in this context that we begin our brief study of the early development of the fighting knife on a world-wide basis.

Among the first so-called fighting knives were those crafted by the Egyptians, approximately 3500 B.C. These were followed by the bronze daggers of the Sumerians in about 2500 B.C., and those of the Scandanavians, which appeared during the great ''Dagger Period'' of 1800-1500 B.C.

The Hittites are credited with the first iron-bladed fighting knives, which made their appearance c. 1500 B.C. The Hittite methods of blade-smithing were subsequently lost to the Philistines, and then to the Jews, in the period from 1025 to 975 B.C. By 700 B.C., iron daggers and fighting knives had extended to both Greece and Egypt, and within the next century, to Britain and India.

In about 400 B.C., the double-edged dagger began to die out, to be replaced by the single-edged knife. The popularity of both dagger and fighting knife continued to decline until the 9th and 10th centuries A.D., when they were revived by the Viking culture. Part of the reason for this decline was the forenamed introduction of the single-edged blade, which relegated the knife to more utilitarian purposes.

In spite of this, it was through the agency of one particular single-edged weapon that fighting knives once again ascended to general favor. This weapon was the Viking *scramasax,* a very formidable instrument, thought by many to be the ancient ancestor of the Bowie knife. The scramasax proved to be among the world's most popular fighting knives until the beginning of the Middle Ages.

Thereafter, during the period of about 1200 to 1500 A.D., seven major dagger families made their appearance. Of these, Peterson has characterized the *Rondel, Baselard, Quillion Dagger, Ballock Knife, Earred Dagger* and *Cinequeda* as the most influential types.

The 17th century saw the introduction of the bayonet, with the dirk following in the 18th century. To the 19th century we owe that prince of fighting blades, the Bowie knife; in its first or earliest form, more of a short sword than a true knife.

Thus it is that the fighting knife, or dagger, possesses within itself a history reaching back almost eighty centuries. A proper appreciation of this history is essential to any study of the fighting blade, especially because we are now (and have been for the past three centuries), in an era of derivative design. Although many modifications and minor refinements have been made in the past — and continue to be made in the present — in a very general sense, nothing really new has been introduced to the design of fighting knives in at least a century.

TOOLS OF THE TRADE

While it is not the primary purpose of this book to give an exhaustive study of fighting knife development, it is central to our purposes to provide a sound overview of the "tools of the trade." To accomplish this, we will place our principal emphasis upon present day knives which have —

1. had a profound effect upon the means by which the art of knife fighting is taught;

2. had a profound effect upon the design of later fighting knives, in general.

It may be said that the whole of current fighting knife design revolves around two basic types, or styles, which in themselves owe their greater origins to antiquity: the Fairbairn-Sykes Fighting Knife, and the Bowie knife.

To be sure, there are such types as the U.S. Mark III trench knife, the Mark I trench knife, the Gurkha *kukri* and others, but the Fairbairn-Sykes and the Bowie still continue to exert the greatest influence over both the design of fighting knives, and the practice of knife fighting.

The Fairbairn-Sykes

Until quite recently, the F-S Fighting Knife was thought by many to be the ultimate in fighting knife design. Of course, we are immediately troubled by nomenclature here, as the F-S is, more accurately, a fighting *dagger* rather than a fighting knife.

Originally developed by W.E. Fairbairn and E.A. Sykes for the use of the British Combined Operations Command, this weapon was also briefly issued to operatives of the Office of Strategic Services, and to members of the American forces (designated variously as the V-42, which was used by the 1st S.S.F., and the ''Camillus Stiletto,'' issued to Marine units in 1943). The F-S reached its greatest level of popularity during World War II, and has lately enjoyed a good deal of recognition from the Studies and Observation Groups of the 5th Special Forces.

In its first, or purest form, the F-S was an excellent weapon indeed. The author's own specimen, acquired by way of a former O.S.S. operative, is a notable example. Originally issued to a member of the No. 6 Commando (a group which served with distinction in the long-remembered Raid of Vaagso, Norway, December, 1941), it is of the type manufactured in Britain during the very early stages of the war; probably about 1940. The handle is of brass, bearing the rare form of ''beads and ridges'' tooling; the blade is blued, and the weapon is perfectly balanced. This knife is, no doubt, a perfect example of what Fairbairn and Sykes had in mind when the weapon was designed. There is evidence which leads one to believe that this particular specimen is from a lot manufactured under Fairbairn's direct supervision.

The Fairbairn-Sykes rapidly deteriorated from this ideal form, however, as brass was quickly found to be a strategic material. Later handles were fashioned of aluminum, wood, and in certain cases, even leather. With this change in handle material naturally came a change in the weapon's weight. As a result, later examples of the F-S will often have a severe balance problem. Indeed, although the original specifications for this weapon called for an over-all weight of

Figure 14   Figure 15

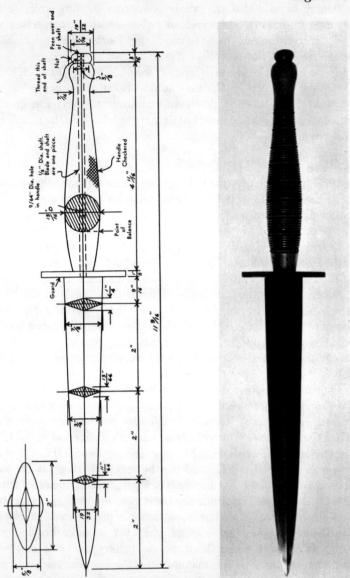

The original design for the Fairbairn-Sykes Fighting Knife; developed at the Commando Special Training Center in Achnacarry, Scotland by W.E. Fairbairn and E.A. Sykes. (reprinted from *Kill or Get Killed*, Copyright (C) 1961 The Stackpole Company, Used Here by Permission).

The rare "beads and ridges" form of the Fairbairn-Sykes, manufactured during the early stages of World War II. (Author's collection)

but six ounces, the author has examined supposedly ''original'' models weighing up to a pound!

Fairbairn no doubt designed this weapon with the fencing foil in mind, in keeping with his ideas of a darting, thrusting, parrying knife attack. Were knife fighting confined to two-man frontal assault situations, the F-S would rank among the world's most efficient weapons. But most knife fighting is not a man-to-man practice, and the F-S has therefore, been found to be somewhat limited in application. In addition, a number of design defficiencies have been discovered during the years of its use.

Points to consider in choosing the F-S as your weapon are as follows:

1. The blade is long, slim, and sharply tapered to an extreme point, thus rendering it liable to breakage.

2. The blade of the F-S is of the ''round tang'' design, which may, in certain cases, result in weakness at the junction of blade and handle.

3. The weapon's handle is cylindrical, and difficult to orient in the hand by ''feel'' or tactile sense. This cylindrical design also makes the knife subject to twisting or rolling from the hand.

4. The knife bears a cross-guard, which can be snagged on clothing during penetration or withdrawal.

The above is, by no means, meant to read as an indictment of the F-S. Rather than follow the normal course of presentation favored by most guides, and present a weapon only in its most favorable light, the author believes it will better serve the interests of the reader if a point is made of these defficiencies, rather than ignoring them altogether. After all, you may one day stake your *life* on this weapon. If you do, it is best to have some idea of the weapon's limitations firmly in mind, so you will not expect the impossible.

The F-S has directly influenced a number of other fighting knives. Among these are several of the all-purpose combat knives made by today's cutlery manufacturers and custom knifemakers.

A particularly excellent fighting/survival knife which has a great deal in common with the F-S is Gerber's *Mark II*, designed by Mr. Al Mar, resident design engineer with Gerber Legendary Blades, Portland, Oregon. The Gerber Mark II is made from the low-alloy grade L6 tool steel also known as Reading Double Service Steel, and shipped from the factory with a relative hardness of approximately 58 on the Rockwell ''C'' scale. The handle, which is semi-cylindrical, is covered with a ground thermosetting vinyl material, and is permanently bonded to the blade's tang.

Figure 16

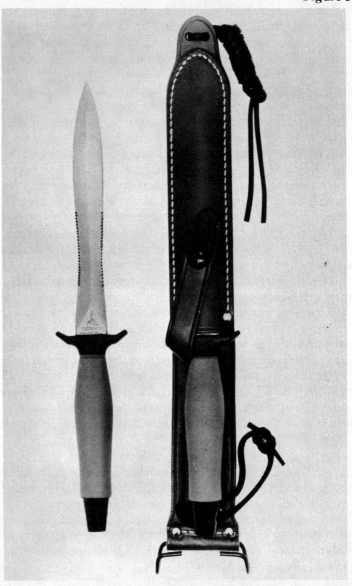

The Gerber Mark II Fighting Survival Knife. A great favorite among
U.S. troops overseas and at home. (Knife Digest Photo)

While not a true Fairbairn-Sykes in the strictest sense (the blade possesses a series of saw-teeth), the influence is nonetheless apparent. The Mark II became a great favorite of ground troops during the Vietnam conflict, and continues to be a popular choice among servicemen. At a retail price of approximately $45., the author believes the Mark II to represent a good value, and is thus able to recommend its purchase.

Among custom knifemakers, John Cooper, W.D. Randall, Jr., John Smith, James Lile and Ralph Bone have all crafted blades influenced by the Fairbairn-Sykes. In each case, however, these custom-crafted blades will bear the mark of the maker's own ideas regarding the perfect knife. Because of this, the interested reader is advised to shop around.

One final word about the Fairbairn-Sykes: numerous published references have termed the F-S as "Sykes-Fairbairn," "Fairbirn, Fairborn, Fairbern Knife," and etcetera. In his book *Get Tough!*, Major Fairbairn termed his blade the *Fairbairn-Sykes Fighting Knife.* We have accepted Major Fairbairn as the best possible authority.

The Bowie Knife

Modern edged weapons historians now believe that the Bowie knife was not original with James Bowie. Rather, it was the Bowie family's interpretation of a much earlier form of fighting knife: the so-called Spanish Dagger.

The false edge and double quillion guard which we have come to associate with the typical Bowie knife are thought to have been introduced by a cutler named Henry Schively, who worked in Philadelphia, Pennsylvania during the 1820's and 1830's.

In the words of Bowie biographer Lucy Bowie, writing in 1916:

"In 1832, the brothers went North. Rezin wished to consult the celebrated Doctor Pepper, of Philadelphia about his eyes. On that same northern trip he gave into the hands of a Philadelphia cutler the model of the Bowie knife. The cutler improved it and placed them on the market. The blade was shortened to eight inches; a curve was made in one side of the point and both edges were sometimes sharpened."

According to theory, Schively was the cutler visited by James Bowie's brother Rezin on that trip to Philadelphia. This theory is based on the fact that Dr. Pepper's office was located at number 225 Chestnut Street, Philadelphia, while Henry Schively's shop was located at number 75 Chestnut Street.

But no matter who is responsible for the ''invention'' of the Bowie knife, it has certainly endured to become America's most influential

Figure 17

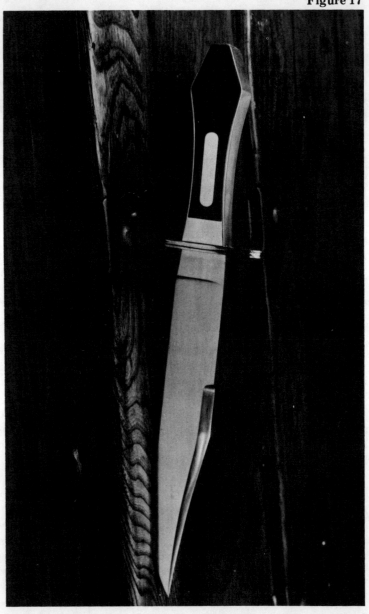

This is a modern reproduction of a relatively late form of Bowie knife; one which exhibits English influence by virtue of its "coffin handle." (Knife Digest Photo)

Figure 18

Figure 18

Figure 19

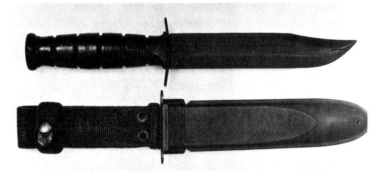

Figure 20

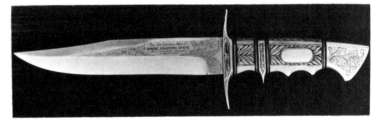

The weapon pictured here was made by custom knifemaker Bob Dozier to resemble a typical Bowie knife of the 1830-1850 era. It is this style that collectors have come to regard as "classic." (Knife Digest Photo)

The "KA-BAR" fighting-utility knife, much favored by American forces since World War II. Shown here with type MK-2 scabbard. (Knife Digest Photo)

The first of the modern sub-hilt fighting knives, made in 1957 by noted custom knifemaker Robert W. Loveless. Loveless pioneered the sub-hilt treatment, but has abandoned the Bowie blade style illustrated here for the "dual grind" form shown elsewhere (Photo courtesy R.W. Loveless)

edged weapon. During the period of its most frequent use, and well into the Civil War years, the Bowie was highly prized as a fighting knife by scores of combatants. Over the course of these years the Bowie developed into a form which we have come to regard as typical: a heavy bladed weapon, approximately a foot in length; bearing cross-guard and clip point; used for stabbing, thrusting, and the over-hand slash.

Among latter day fighting knives which have been influenced by the Bowie are such famous makes as the Randall Model 1; Randall Model 14; Loveless 6½'' Fighting Knife; Dan Dennehy's Green Beret Model; the Navy's Mark II; and the U.S. Marine Corps' fighting-utility knife. (Better known as the ''KA-BAR,'' after the tang-mark of its maker, the Union Cutlery Company.)

Another fighting knife which may be thought of as Bowie influenced — although not in the strict Bowie style — is the combat and survival weapon manufactured for Argentina's forces. Marked *Fabrica Militar De Armas Portatiles ''DM'' Rosario D.G.F.M. Industria Argentina,* this particular knife must certainly rank among the world's best military designs. This knife has a serious draw-back, however: it is a bit heavy in the handle, owing to the formidable ''skull-crusher'' affixed to the pommel. Otherwise, the Argentine knife is an excellent weapon in many respects.

How efficient is the Bowie style when it comes to actual use? This is a question which has plagued experts for years. To some, the Bowie is much too limited a design to be a truly effective fighting weapon. Others swear by it, and would possess no other form of blade.

Much of the criticism of the Bowie revolves around its clip point, and the fact that the average Bowie knife is best held via the Hammer Grip (see Part III: Tactics). This, it is felt, severely limits its maneuverability. It is also believed that the clip point makes it difficult to instinctively direct precision thrusts — whether in the dark, or in the heat of battle — as the tip of the point seems ''lower'' than it actually is.

Another criticism is the Bowie's sharpening scheme: the knife is sharpened on but a single edge. At least one maker, Robert W. Loveless, of Riverside, California, solved this problem by sharpening both edges of his Bowie-influenced fighting knife all the way back to the hilt. The Loveless Fighting Knife was designed according to the principles of use set forth in Styers' *Cold Steel,* and as such, it is an' extremely popular weapon among knowledgeable users.

The above criticisms notwithstanding, Bowie Knives remain the first choice of countless knife fighters the world over. Perhaps this is a result of the Bowie style's reputation for dependability, as well as the reputation of its most famous wielder.

MISCELLANEOUS TYPES

There is another class of fighting knife which bears no resemblance to either the Fairbairn-Sykes or the Bowie. Among these we find many and diverse attempts at the ideal fighting weapon; products of man's never-ending struggle to "build a better mouse-trap." In order to completely familiarize the reader with as many different fighting knives as is possible, we will here examine a few of the more notable types, which we have characterized as "miscellaneous."

Knuckle Knives

With the advent of World War I, there came a reawakening of interest in the fighting knife; doubtless inspired by the terrible spectre of trench warfare. This renewed interest led to the development of America's intriguing Model 1917 trench knife, designed by the Henry Disston & Sons firm, of Philadelphia.

The Model 1917 (and the later Model 1918 — virtually identical in design), was restricted to use as a stabbing weapon. Its nine-inch blade was triangular, much like a file, and tapered narrowly to an extreme point. This point, it is noted, frequently broke in the heat of battle.

The knuckle-bow of the Model 1917 strongly resembled that of a cutlass. This "cutlass bow" was modified by a series of pyramidal knobs, intended to have lethal effect.

The problem with the 1917 and 1918 trench knives stemmed from the fact that they could be grasped in only one of but two ways: the Ice-Pick Grip, or the Hammer Grip (see Part III: Tactics). To change his grip, the soldier was required to release his weapon altogether!

The model 1917 and Model 1918 trench knives were never very highly regarded by the troops who were forced to use them, and production was curtailed after approximately 123,000 were made.

The Mark I

By the summer of 1918, it was apparent that the Model 1917 and Model 1918 trench knives were a dismal failure. Accordingly, on June 1, 1918, the American Expeditionary Forces conducted a series of tests in order to evaluate the several different trench knife designs then in use. As a result, and with the cooperation of the Ordnance Department, the A.E.F. designed the Mark I trench knife.

Figure 21

Figure 22

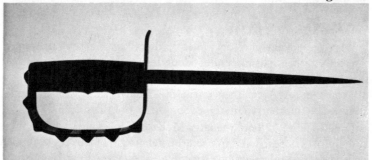

Figure 23

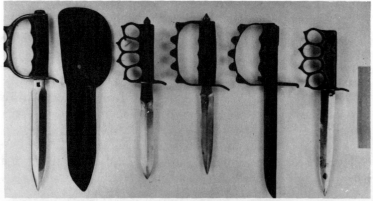

The justly famous California style dirk-knife of noted San Francisco maker Michael Price. This knife was made circa 1860, and is of a type popular with early-day duellists. (Author's collection)

The model 1917 Trench Knife, shown here virtually silhouette to emphasize triangular blade form. (Author's collection)

Five typical "knuckle knives" of the first and second World Wars. All serve to illustrate this particular style's limitations with regard to grip. (Knife Digest Photo)

The Mark I was, actually, borrowed from the French, who had enjoyed some success with a similar design. Indeed, the first Mark I trench knives were procured from a French manufacturer. Later knives were manufactured by the U.S. firm of Landers, Frary and Clark. Due to the Armistice, L.F. & C. was only able to manufacture approximately 120,000 of these knives before all orders were cancelled. As a side note: although it did not see widespread use during World War II, the Mark I was not declared obsolete until January, 1945.

Like the Model 1917 and Model 1918, the Mark I was a knuckle knife: in this case, the knuckles being cast of bronze rather than stamped from sheet iron. The finger grips were contoured, much in the manner of typical "brass knucks," and there was a sharp nut at the pommel.

If the Model 1917 was limited in application, the Mark I was even more-so! Although the blade had been changed from triangular to a more conventional dagger form, the soldier was still prevented from using the blade to its maximum potential by the confining handle design. As with the Model 1917, the Mark I's advantages were largely psychological, and the weapon was never widely used.

Despite the acknowledged limitations of knuckle knives as effective fighting weapons, they still persist. Among later forms are the knives of the 1st Ranger Battalion, and the countless "home-made" jobs which have found their way to the front lines of every conflict from Korea to Cambodia. The serious knife figher is cautioned against their use, as they are better kept for collection, and are today highly prized.

The Mark III

"The Trench Knife M3 has been developed to fill the need in modern warfare for hand-to-hand fighting. While designated for issue to soldiers not armed with the bayonet, it was especially designed for such shock units as parachute troops and rangers."

Thus the *Catalog of Standard Ordnance Items* heralded the development of America's M3 trench knife. Production of this slim fighting blade began in 1943, and continues, in limited quantities, to the present. (In actual issue it has largely been supplanted by the bayonet-knife M4.)

Unlike its predecessors, the M3 is not encumbered by either knuckle grips or overly-radical blade form. The M3 is a more or less conventional dagger-like weapon, owing much to the Fairbairn-Sykes school of design. The M3 has a cylindrical handle and straight false edge, ground back 2 3/4" from the point. The bottom edge is ground all the way to the hilt.

Figure 24

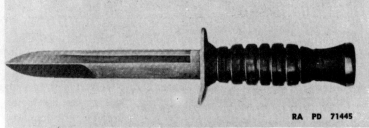

RA PD 71445

Illustration of "Knife, Trench, M3" as depicted in Army Service Forces Catalog, March 24, 1944. Knife is unaccountably pictured upside-down.

The M3 is a fighting weapon, of that we can be certain, and has certain points to recommend itself. By the same token, it has certain design points which may be thought of as possible defficiencies.

One wonders why the top edge is ground back for so brief a distance, and also why the blade is so thin. With a partial grind, the blade is somewhat limited in multiple slash situations, and again, being thin the blade is liable to breakage. As with the F-S, the M3 also has the problems of cylindrical handle and cross-guard. In addition to the above, the M3 as issued does not take the keenest edge.

Custom Knives

Since the late 1960's, there has been a marked increase in the number of "custom," or one-of-a-kind, hand-made knives. The custom knifemakers now form a very vocal and influential minority of the cutlery industry, and many of their designs are finding acceptance by major manufacturers.

Many readers will no doubt be familiar with such well-known custom knifemakers as W.D. "Bo" Randall, Jr., of Orlando, Florida, and Robert W. Loveless, former president of the prestigious Knifemakers Guild — a fraternal and professional organization of custom knifemakers. However, for those of you who have, as yet, had no experience with custom knifemaking, the author can suggest no better introduction than the *Knifemakers Guild Directory of the Membership*, available for $3.00 through R.W. Loveless, P.O. Box 7836, Riverside, California 92503.

This 105 page book (for which the author was privileged to write an introduction), lists every member of the Knifemakers Guild, illustrates popular models of their various knives, and gives you full information regarding where you may write for catalogs and price-lists.

Besides the Randall and Loveless knives previously recommended, the reader is advised to seriously investigate the knives of two other makers: Dan Dennehy, of Yuma, Arizona, and Walter "Blackie" Collins, of Rock Hill, South Carolina.

Figure 25

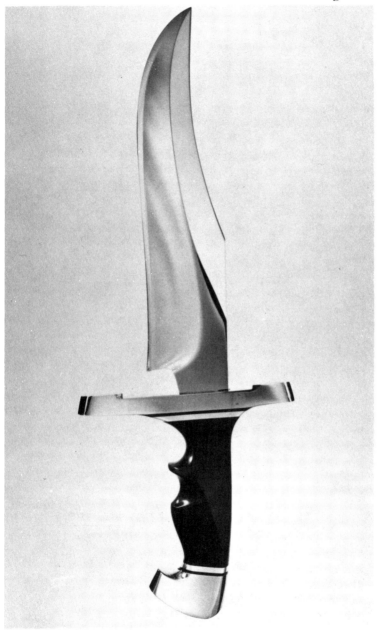

Custom knifemaker Roderick Caribou Chappel's "Karate Knife." An extremely radical design — not for everyone — but definitely worthy of notice. (Knife Digest Photo)

Figure 27

The first — and many
think the best — of
the modern fighting
knives,
handmade by
"Bo" Randall, Jr.,
the acknowledged
"Dean" of
custom knifemaking.

Shown here are
Model 1 and
Model 2
eight-inch
fighting weapons;
two designs which
have proved
themselves
in battle
time and time again.

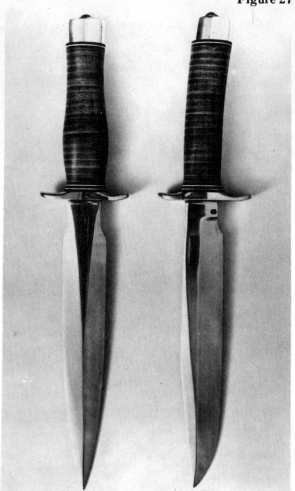

(Photo courtesy
W.D. Randall, Jr.)

Figure 26

Cover of the *Knifemakers Guild Directory of the Membership*. Book is a
valuable introduction to custom knifemaking. (Photo courtesy The
Knifemakers Guild)

The author's favorite Randall-Made knife: the 7½ inch Model 14 "Attack". It has been said, and rightfully so, that no serious knife fighter's armory is complete without a Randall knife. (Photo courtesy W.D. Randall, Jr.)

Figure 28

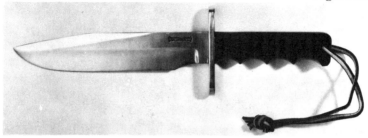

Figure 29

A case of fighting daggers by custom knifemaker John Cooper, of Burbank, California. Primarily for the collector, this case of blades might also serve an extremely belligerant knife fighter! (Knife Digest Photo)

Figure 30

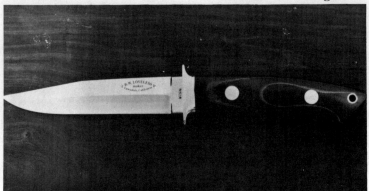

A current-production five inch boot knife by R.W. Loveless.

Many veterans of the Pacific theatre in World War II may recall purchasing knives from then-Chief Petty Officer Dan Dennehy, who has since retired from the Navy to pursue the knifemaking profession in earnest. Dennehy's Recon Special model is a particular favorite with many service personnel, and warmly recommended.

"Blackie" Collins will be instantly recognized by many readers as Smith & Wesson's resident cutlery designer. Mr. Collins also has the distinction of being America's most prolific creator of patentable cutlery designs; at present holding over thirty U.S. patents. By virtue of his work with both Smith & Wesson and the military, Mr. Collins' knives are also recommended.

Switchblades

Senator Kefauver to the contrary, the switchblade, gravity knife, or spring-driven folding knife is not a very effective combat weapon. If anything, they are more suited to theatrical purposes than conflict. Federal legislation banning their use is much like Gun Control: restrictive, rather than beneficial. Switchblades may be easily thought of as the "Saturday Night Specials" of the cutlery world — a token piece of less than desirable meat thrown to a pack of howling wolves.

A spring-driven blade ("spring-driven" here to mean a blade which is opened by releasing a spring under tension), does not make a spring-back folding knife any more or less deadly than it already is. ("Spring-back" here to mean all common folding knives.) The only viable distinction between folding knives which may be used as weapons and folding knives which may not, has to do with whether or not the knife's blade may be locked in the open position.

The common switchblade, as currently manufactured in Italy, Japan, Germany, and, in certain cases, the United States, does not possess a truly servicable locking mechanism. By and large, these locking mechanisms are of the "blockage" variety, i.e. a lock prevents the push-button from releasing the blade. To be completely safe, a locking mechanism must *positively* affect both the blade and the back-spring, rather than operating on a chain effect, or a cam principle.

The next problem of many switchblades has to do with weak or easily broken spring mechanisms, many of which are inclined to be a conglomeration of many small components. Add to this the amount of care needed to keep a switchblade in top working order: even the slightest pocket trash, bits of brush, or other intrusions can be enough to foul the best-quality switchblade.

Most switchblade drive-springs are of undesirable quality, being batch tempered and of a poor grade of steel. Often they are bent, or

A page from the Norvell-Shapleigh Hardware Company's knife catalog of 1910, illustrating the component parts of a common switchblade.

Cut Shows Full View of Knife with Sections of Coverings Removed.

Safety Slides Released, Allowing Blades to Open when Buttons are Pressed.

Fig. 7—Showing Black Celluloid Covering Removed

Fig. 8—Locking Device which slides under the Button

Fig. 9—Spring which throws the Lever, Locking the Blade

Fig. 10—Shows Locking Lever
Fig. 11—Shows the Brass Lining of the Knife with Rivet Perforations

Fig. 12—Back Spring of the Knife

Fig. 13—Fly Spring which throws open either Blade
Fig. 14—Reverse Lock for the Second Blade in the Knife
Fig. 15—The Spring for Locking the Lever

Fig. 16—Solid Rivet Running through Covering, Blade and Lining of Knife
Fig. 17—Hollow Rivets, going through Blades as well as Linings of Knives (extra Strengthening to Knife)

Fig. 18—Second Black Celluloid Covering or Handle of Knife, showing Depressions for Locking Device

Fig. 19—Showing Scale cut off for a Tipped or Bolstered Knife—Depressions showing the place for the Mechanism of the Locking Device

Fig. 20—Locking Lever for Blade
Fig. 21—Button for releasing Lock of Blade
Fig. 22—Sliding Locking Device
Fig. 23—Tips or German Silver Bolsters for Knives

Fig. 24—Showing enlarged Solid Rivet and adding extra strength to Knife No other Spring Knife made in this way
Fig. 25—Solid Rivet running through Covering, Blade and Lining of Knife
Fig. 26—Showing Press Button, releasing Lock or Lever
Fig. 27—Showing enlarged Locking Device
Fig. 28—Shows Lever Locking Spring
Fig. 29—Showing enlarged Locking Lever

Figure 31

Figure 32

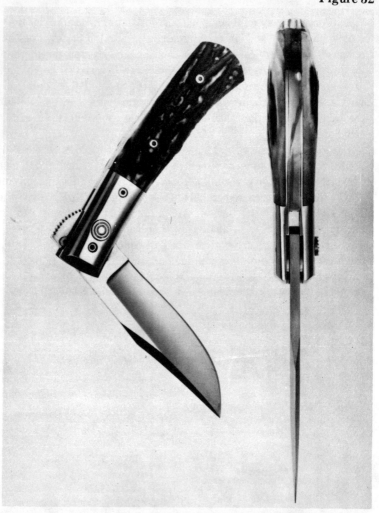

Two custom folding knives by a maker no longer in business. Any folding knife, no matter how simple or complex, is a poor second to the fixed-blade fighting knife. (Knife Digest Photo)

canted, at a bad angle, to the point where frequent use causes the spring to rupture and break at the stress point. For the most part, switchblade springs examined by the author suffered from being too flimsy, with a resulting lack of power, or too heavy, and improperly tempered for their volume. It must also be remembered that the typical switchblade has but one blade, and thus the width allowance for the drive-spring is quite small.

Should you use a switchblade for combat purposes? Only if you're dealing with an adversary who is easily impressed, and there is no other weapon handy. Strange as it may seem, the switchblade is a very poor weapon: a device better suited to the parachutist or agriculturist than the knife fighter.

Folding Knives

The problem with non-switchblade type folding knives is one of *time.* It requires two moves to get the average well-made folding knife into action, and for many of us, it's not worth the added effort. First, you have to retrieve the folder from the pocket; second, you have to open it with your free hand. No matter how quickly you can make this move, it is a poor second to quickly pulling a fixed-blade knife from a speed-break sheath.

As before, unless you have a truly solid locking mechanism, you're asking for real trouble. There is nothing worse than a folding knife which unexpectedly closes, as the author knows from bitter, personal experience. To the serious knife fighter, pocketknives or folding knives are best left in the pocket, and should be used only when there is no other edged weapon available.

If you are forced to bring a folding knife into play, unless it's one you have confidence in, the author advises you to confine your moves to upward, sweeping slashes. Do *not* rely on either the blade's lock or joint. A blade which closes on the fingers of the wielder during a thrust or slash has the effect of paralyzing the hand, as the blade will almost invariably sever at least one of the finger tendons. In this case, the knife would drop from your crippled hand, and you would find yourself at the mercy of your enemy.

The Push Dirk

Push dirks (or ''push daggers'' as they are sometimes improperly termed), were a popular weapon of America's frontier days; principally used by riverboat gamblers and waterfront thugs. They are possibly East Indian in origin, and came to this country by way of the French cutlers of old New Orleans. Today, they have their counterpart in the ''buckle-knife'' designed by Walter ''Blackie'' Collins, the noted edged weapons designer from South Carolina.

The push dirk is used with a short, punching stab, and is thus severely limited in application. The knife fighter may, however, desire to carry one as a back-up to his main blade. In its buckle-knife form, the push dirk is quite popular with law enforcement personnel, and those who frequently find themselves in dangerous urban situations.

Figure 33

A typical push dirk by early California knifemaker Michael Price.
(Collection of Peter Buxtun)

Boot and Sleeve Knives

The boot and sleeve knives, each requiring their own special sheath equipment, are becoming increasingly popular. Virtually every custom knifemaker in the United States now offers a version of the ''hide-out'' knife, at prices ranging from fifty to five hundred dollars.

Among the best of these are the boot and sleeve knives hand made by the Morseth firm, of Springdale, Arkansas. The Morseth boot knife has a 4½'' blade, is available with a variety of handle materials, and comes complete with a ''speed-break'' sheath. This sheath may either be attached to the belt, or affixed to the inside of the boot by means of Velcro strips. The author has carried this knife for a number of years now, and it well satisfied with its performance.

The Morseth sleeve knife comes complete with but one variety of sheath, that being a straight pouch type, which is held in place by Velcro. The blade of this knife is a rather stubby dagger type, and is best suited to use as a stabbing weapon. This particular knife sells for around sixty dollars.

Generally speaking, boot and sleeve knives are recommended as a back-up weapon. It should be remembered that they are not exclusively designed for combat use, being, by their very nature, rather small and compact. Still, they are an excellent choice for street wear, or similar situations where small, easily concealable knives are indicated.

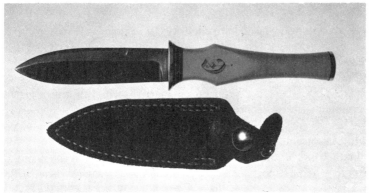

Figure 34

Author's own boot knife, shown here with "speed-break" sheath, set up for belt wear. Knife is manufactured by the Morseth firm, in Springdale, Arkansas. (Author's collection)

Figure 35

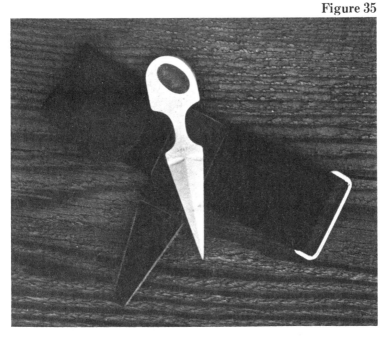

This is but one example of the wrist, or sleeve style knife. Knife here shown is no longer in production. (Knife Digest Photo)

The Kukri and the Kris

A word should be said here about two very popular Asian knives; the *kukri* (pronounced "kook-ree"), and the *kris* (pronounced "Kreease").

The kukri is the favored weapon of Nepal's Gurkha tribe, and has ascended to a great degree of popularity owing to the legends surrounding its use. Contrary to popular belief, however, the kukri is a rather recent development in Northern Indian edged weaponry, owing its origins to approximately the 18th century.

In the hands of the Gurkha, the kukri is used much in the manner of an intrenching tool, and also as a decapitating weapon. Its curved, swelling blade makes it unsuitable for all but the swinging chop, or slash. In Nepal today, one sees the kukri worn with its scabbard extending down the left side of the body — frequently beneath the waistband — its hilt roughly to the right-center of the wearer's stomach. From this position the kukri is drawn with a peculiar upward slice to the victim's throat. Although a formidable weapon in Asia, particularly in Nepal, the kukri is not well suited to modern knife fighting.

As to the kris: several works have been written on this weapon of Indonesia, mostly notably, Donn F. Draegar's *Weapons & Fighting Arts of the Indonesian Archipelagos.* As Mr. Draegar is the world's greatest English language authority on the subject of Asian fighting arts, the interested reader is directed to his book for further study.

The kris is a highly evolved weapon, considering its polyglot origins, and with minor modifications of grip, could become an excellent choice for modern knife fighting.

The kris, as it is usually encountered, has a blade ranging in length from ten to seventeen inches, and is frequently formed from meteorite iron. Two basic blade styles are known: the "wavy" form, bearing up to seven radical curves along its edges, and the "arc" form, which is a great deal more common. This last style has a gradual downward curve along its entire length, and is the style best suited to modern use.

Kris fittings and hilt furniture are frequently very ornate, and are fashioned variously of bone, horn (the most common), precious woods, and thin metal. The scabbard of the typical kris has a feature known as the "boat" which is used to secure the weapon to the wearer's waist by means of a sash or cord. These "boats" are frequently decorated with a very high degree of intricate carving, as are the hilts.

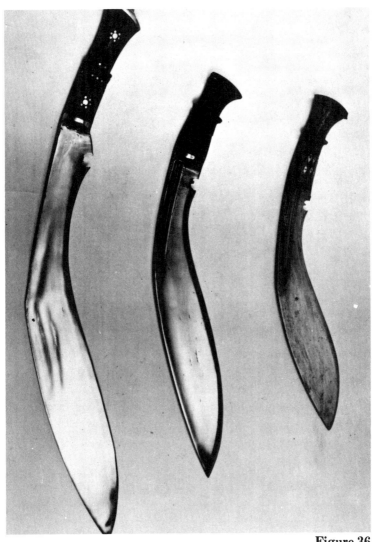

Figure 36

The Gurkha *kukri;* an 18th century development in Nepalese weaponry. Center specimen is, perhaps, the more typical form. (Photo courtesy Dr. Luis Blanco-Hernandez)

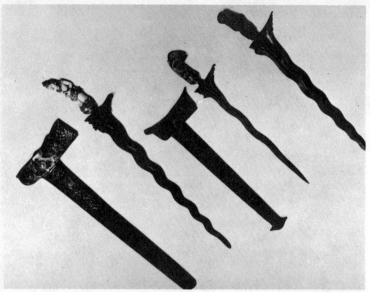

Figure 37

The ornate form of Indonesia's *kris*, illustrated here with "wavy" blade style. Although unconventional to Western eyes, in the hands of a skilled user the *kris* is a formidable weapon. (Photo courtesy Dr. Luis Blanco-Hernandez)

The Tactical-Survivor

We come now the last fighting knife to be considered in this study, one which was designed by the author, and one which is now enjoying a certain degree of acceptance from various world military forces.

Possessing a knowledge of the various difficulties encountered with other knife designs, and in an attempt to put theory into practice, the author has developed a combination fighting/survival knife designated the "Cassidy Tactical-Survivor Combat Knife."

At present, prototypes of this weapon are being seriously considered by the procurement officers of two foreign nations, and as of this writing, a third foreign government has authorized procurement for experimental issue to special intelligence units. It is doubtful that this mass-produced military version of the Cassidy Tactical-Survivor will ever be obtainable by non-military personnel.

There is, however, a completely hand-made version which is available to civilians. Anticipating civilian interest in this weapon, the author has granted a license to make the Tactical-Survivor to custom knifemaker Blackie Collins. This particular model, which is illustrated in the accompanying photographs, sells for seventy-five

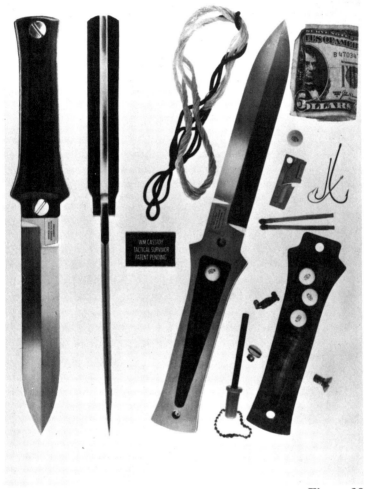

Figure 38

The Cassidy Tactical-Survivor. Weight fully assembled is 12 ounces; over-all length is 12 inches; blade length is 6-3/8 inches blade width is 1-1/8 inches; blade stock is 1/4 inch; handles are of black Micarta. Version here shown is available for civilian purchase. (Author's collection)

dollars. The only design difference between this version and the mass-produced version has to do with the method of affixing the special handle-scales. On the military version, the handles bear a quick-release latching mechanism. The hand-made model bears short-throw, coin-slotted screws.

The blade of the Tactical-Survivor is an improved "four-grind" type. It presents an effective cutting surface of six inches on the bottom edge and five and one-half inches on the top edge. This grind lends balance to the center of the weapon, added strength at this balance, or control point, and provides for ease in rapid manufacture.

The blade is a full one and one-quarter inches wide, and possesses but one inch of "taper" to the point. This one inch taper is particularly critical to the knife's function as a weapon, in that it provides for ease of penetration and withdrawal, and its function as a utilitarian tool is vastly improved. It should also be added that the blade is ground and machined from quarter-inch stock, rather than the more common three-sixteenths. As the Cassidy Tactical-Survivor may be applied to rough use, the added strength this provides is well worth the added expense in manufacture.

When used as a thrusting weapon, initial resistance to penetration is absorbed immediately upon striking, due to the short taper point design. Secondary resistance to penetration is eliminated, as the first inch of blade rapidly establishes a drag-free full blade-width entry wound. Full-length taper blades often present tissue resistance, or "drag" along their entire length, as they present a consistently wider surface from point to hilt. In addition, their radically tapered points often prevent easy withdrawal, due to the point becoming momentarily "frozen" when bone is struck. The blade of the Cassidy Tactical-Survivor presents none of these problems. As it is sharpened on both edges, it may also be used to effect both right and left-hand slashes, according to the approved technique of modern knife fighting.

The Tactical-Survivor utilizes scale-tang construction, and thus provides for a unique method of "cavity-handle" design. Due to its novel outline, this cavity-handle presents none of the structural weaknesses of tubular hollow-handle, or slot-handle designs. When the knife is completely disassembled, the special design of the tang cavity allows the knife to be used as a pry bar, bottle opener, or emergency wrench. The knife will handle any bolt from seven-eights to one quarter of an inch.

In addition to the abilities common to any well-designed survival weapon; such as storage, suitability for lashing to a pole, or use in a man-trap, the Cassidy Tactical-Survivor also bears removable handle scales. While essential to the knife's over-all design, these removable scales have an added benefit: they provide the opportunity for substitution of material without requiring extensive re-design. They may be fashioned of wood, aluminum, high-impact plastic, vulcanized rubber, fibre, or resin-impregnated cloth. Any material which can be molded, turned, shaped, or cast is ideal for the Tactical-Survivor.

The basic shape of the Tactical-Survivor's handle promotes correct grip and deft handling. It is possible to quickly orient the blade in the hand in total darkness, strictly by ''feel'' or tactile sense. The handle design also acts as a safety device, in that it prevents against the hand slipping down the knife and being cut on the blade. Conversely, it is also extremely difficult to pull the knife from the hand, when the correct grip on the handle is maintained. The handle's over-all shape. helps guard against the knife dropping when wet, or rolling from the hand in combat situations.

Currently, many different design improvements are being incorporated into the Cassidy Tactical-Survivor; such improvements as bead-blasting the blade to guard against reflection without the problems of bluing or parkerizing, and special forms of checkering and surfacing for the handle scales. The basic idea of the knife, however, remains the same, with U.S. and world patents pending.

There are also plans to offer a scaled down version of this knife, suitable for wear in the boot or within the sleeve, designated the ''Cassidy Strategic-Survivor.'' Readers who may be interested in obtaining the Tactical-Survivor or the Strategic-Survivor are advised to contact MEWD Corp., P.O. Box 4596, Sather Gate Station, Berkeley, California 94704. ''MEWD'' is the acronym for Military Edged Weapons Development Corporation, for which the author serves as a consultant and designer.

CONCEALMENT AND METHODS OF CARRY

How best to carry the fighting knife you have chosen? To most of us, this question is easily answered by personal preference. There is, however, one method of carrying which should be given serious consideration before seeking an alternative.

This method calls for a sheath of specialized design, which may either be affixed to the clothing of the wearer by sewing, or strapped securely in place. We call this method the *Chest Carry.*

With the Chest Carry, the knife is held diagonally across the wielder's chest — across the heart in the case of right-handed persons — the blade pointed over the shoulder and away from the head. In

Figure 39

R.W. Loveless demonstrates the Chest Carry, using special shoulder holster of his own design.

Figure 40

Loveless quickly pulls the knife from the speed-break sheath.

Figure 41

Loveless naturally shifts into Battery Position, with no wasted motion.

this position it requires but a brief, short movement before the knife is in a firm *en garde,* or Battery Position, at the waist. (See Part III: Tactics). Should the wearer be subjected to a fall, or become engaged in an unexpected grapple, he will be in no danger of being injured by his own blade.

This method has the added benefit of making it difficult for an adversary to remove one's knife unassailed. Another benefit is that the knife may be kept concealed beneath a jacket, coat, heavy shirt, or any similar garment. Perhaps the only drawback to this method is that it is not easily used by women, owing to their pleasing anatomy.

A word of caution: when utilizing the Chest Carry, it is important to have a sheath scabbard arrangement which prevents the knife from accidentally dropping, and does not easily snag on brush.

Sheaths and scabbards fall into two basic categories: those with keeper straps, or similar devices, and those with the so-called "speed-break" feature. Sheaths with keeper straps, while the most secure, do not lend themselves well to quick use. Speed-break sheaths, on the other hand, are usually somewhat lacking when it comes to preventing the knife from being accidentally lost. If you do not wish to have a specially designed sheath made, or if cost is a problem, it will then become a question of which feature you feel is most important: speed or security? To the author's way of thinking, the type of sheath or scabbard you choose should depend on the environment in which you contemplate using it. For street, or urban wear, the speed-break sheaths are ideal. For jungle, or diverse combat situations, the most secure sheath will probably be your choice.

Besides the Chest Carry mentioned above, knife fighters have favored every conceivable method of carry from belt to boot, to the back of the neck. Methods of concealment are equally legion. There is a certain problem with concealment, however, and that is *speed.* While the inside of the thigh is, perhaps, an ideal place to hide a blade, it is extremely difficult to get the blade into action from this position. To summarize: no matter where you choose to wear your knife, or how you choose to conceal it, be certain to temper your choice with common sense, rather than fashion. Too many would-be knife users choose methods of concealment and carry on the basis of rumor and fantasy, rather than a serious survey of the knife's intended use and their own safety.

PART III: THE TACTICS

BY WAY OF INTRODUCTION

Knife fighting has nothing of the ''Field of Honor'' about it. It is instead a mean, dirty business that, unfortunately, sometimes needs doing, either in war or on special assignment.

Contrary to persistent, popular belief, knife fighting is not a glamorous face-to-face duel — both opponents of equal height and build, cold of eye and sure of manner, squared off in a jungle clearing at high noon.

Use of the knife is nothing more than an expedient means whereby one man or woman may put an end to another man or woman's life. Let's face it: killing with a knife is what we're talking about. As any experienced combat instructor will tell you, it is best accomplished in darkness, the enemy taken by surprise, and then stabbed in the back.

Backstabbing . . . How distasteful that phrase is to all civilized people. Yet it is the best possible method by which one person may kill another person with a knife. Any man who claims that the prospect of stabbing another human being in the back is not repugnant, either lies to himself or is morally out of joint. Still, it is supposed that there are situations where no other course of action is possible, and thus the action has been justified.

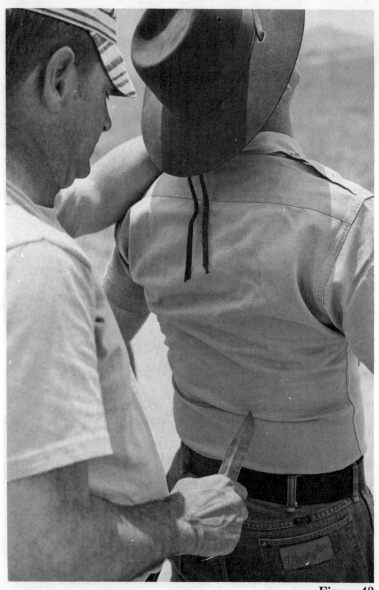

Figure 42

The Sneak Attack. Here our model Bob Loveless directs a thrust to kidney area of model Ray Randall's back; at the same time pulling him backwards into the thrust.

To quickly acclimate the reader to the realities of knife use, and by way of introduction, we will here include a digest of the methods employed in the tactic known as the *Sneak Attack.*

Fairbairn has suggested variations on the sneak attack, all workable, some more-so than others. Applegate has also treated this subject, in greater detail than many of his contemporaries. Various methods are as follows:

1. Strike to the kidneys.
2. Strike to the "small" of the back.
3. Slash or strike to the throat.
4. Strike between collar-bones to Subclavian Artery.
5. Strike to temple.
6. Strike to ear.
7. Strike to eyes or nose.
8. Strike to base of skull.

Among knowledgable backstabbers (and the author will, perhaps, be forgiven his sarcasm at this point) an initial strike to the kidney area(s), followed by an immediate slash to the Carotid Artery (throat) is the method most in vogue. This attack is accomplished as follows:

Drop on your belly, and crawl to a distance of 8 to 10 feet away from the subject, or whatever is practical under the circumstances. This phase of your movement should be accomplished as silently as possible, as your primary goal is to take the subject completely by surprise. Crawling is advocated for the simple reason that you are less likely to be seen, and should some noise betray your movement, a "snap-shot" on the part of the subject will, in many cases, be directed toward an erect target. (Note: To be perfectly objective, we should here mention that the all-fours crawl or belly crawl may not be the best way to approach a subject who is armed with an automatic weapon. Current training demands that such an individual fire an arc burst with his weapon — immediately stepping back — should he for any reason believe he may be molested. Such a burst would have a reasonable chance of striking any immediate target, whether on the ground, crouching, or standing. The counter-move to this would require the attacker to maintain strict silence, and draw the subject's attention to another quarter, by throwing a stone or some similar ruse. It may also be helpful to know that the subject armed with an automatic weapon will be trained to look above the line of his fire, in order to prevent temporary "light blindness" due to the muzzle-flash of his weapon.)

Upon reaching a satisfactory distance behind your enemy, you should rise to a half crouch, swiftly tread a silent step, and then spring upon him with great force. Five feet is the recommended distance from which you should begin this spring. As you strike the

Figure 43

The follow-up to the kidney thrust, as taught to special operatives of America's clandestine services. Knife is pushed forward against the throat, severing the jugular vein.

subject, your left hand should tightly close over his nose and mouth, pulling him backwards, off balance. Simultaneously, with your right hand, you plunge your knife upwards, into the subject's kidney area.

At this point, recommended procedure demands that you count to ten, as steadily as you can, given the circumstances. The knife is then sharply withdrawn, and the throat slashed from ear to ear. An alternative to the slash is a straight stab to a point just beneath the ear, followed by a sawing motion which cuts the throat. Tissue resistance in this area is negligible, and death will occur in approximately twelve to fifteen seconds. This is not a pretty way to kill a man, and is best described as cold-blooded murder. Properly executed, there is absolutely no defense to this form of knife attack.

Historically speaking, knife attacks of this kind have most frequently gone awry due to real or supposed animal cunning, or instinct on the part of the subject, who somehow senses he is being watched. Individuals possessed of this faculty are few and far between. The more common among us suffer from either a lack of training in this faculty, or from dulled senses. Thus, the rearward attack is, more realistically, betrayed by a lack of stealth on the part of the attacker.

BASIC INSTRUCTION

Before continuing with our study of specific tactics, we will now stop and consider the basics of knife fighting. Traditionally, these fundamentals include the study of grip, stance, thrusting and slashing. To these we will append another area of study too long neglected: Mental Discipline.

Grip

Grip is, to a large measure, determined by the particular knife being used. With knives possessed of a cylindrical, or fencing foil-type handle (such as the Fairbairn-Sykes), the so-called *Fence Grip* is employed.

With the Fence Grip, the knife is first laid across the palm; the blade protruding from the thumb side of the hand. The guard of the knife is parallel to the edge of the hand.

Next, the extreme forward portion of the handle — that nearest the guard — is grasped by the thumb and index finger. The thumb is pushed forward, toward the quillion of the guard, and the index finger is curled about the handle, just beneath the thumb. The middle, ring, and small fingers are also curled about the handle. This grip provides for ease of control and extremely deft handling. Control is maintained by the index finger and the thumb, while the middle finger provides for shifts in the position of the blade.

The fighter who utilizes this grip is able to effect right-hand slashes, left-hand slashes, and upward, downward, or straight-in thrusts, much in the manner of the fencer with his foil.

Possible drawbacks to this grip are the unnatural positions to which the wrist is driven when slashing. According to Applegate, when using this grip, the palm should be up and the blade pointed slightly toward the opponent's fore-leg. States Applegate:

"With the palm up it is possible to slash to the right. When the palm is turned down, it is possible to slash to the left."

With the knife held in this position, however, right-hand slashes to the inside of the opponent's left arm, or wrist, require a short, snapping, upward motion, which leaves the knife wielder at a slight disadvantage. To prove this, it is suggested that the reader attempt these slashing movements against an imaginary target, to discover for himself the position to which his wrist and hand will be forced.

The next type of grip is the *Hammer Grip.* According to early accounts, this was the grip most favored by 19th century wielders of the Bowie knife. Historically appealing as this type of grip may be, it is to be shunned by all serious knife fighters. The problem here is that only upward slashes and thrusts may be executed, thus limiting the

Figure 44

Shown here in detail are the Sabre Grip and Complete Grip. (Refer to Figure 8 for demonstration of the Fence Grip). Knife at left is held with the Complete grip. Knife at right is held with the Sabre Grip.

The Hammer Grip in action. Model Ray Randall (at left) is well prepared to launch arm cut against Loveless, who here demonstrates a grip which the intelligent knife fighter must avoid.

Figure 45

Figure 46

Loveless (at right) demonstrates the Ice Pick Grip.

fighter's arsenal of tricks. The Hammer Grip is a frequent choice of the inexperienced or disraught blade wielder.

A variation on the Hammer Grip, and one which possesses none of the latter's weak points, is one where the handle of the knife is held according to the Fence Grip, but the blade is held at right angles to the ground. This is, apparently, the type of grip favored by John Styers.

The Styers Grip represents a vast improvement over the Hammer Grip, and offers additional improvements to the palm-up palm-down grips advocated by Applegate and Fairbairn. With the Styers Grip (usually known as the *Sabre Grip)*, it is possible for the fighter to make better use of the snap thrust — a particular tactic which the seasoned fighter will find most practical.

The third type of grip to be discussed here is really nothing more than an improvement of the Fence Grip. Unlike the Sabre Grip, the blade is held horizontally, rather than vertically. We will call this particular style the *Complete Grip.*

With the Complete Grip, the thumb is placed upon the handle in juxtaposition to the blade, just behind the guard. To quickly visualize this grip, imagine a ''T'' in which the guard forms the cross-stroke,

75

and the thumb forms the descending stroke. With the knife thus grasped, the fighter may execute snap thrusts up, down, to the left and to the right; without the wrist being placed in an unusual or tense position. In addition, with the blade held horizontally, it is somewhat easier to stab an opponent, as the dangers of striking bone or rib are substantially lessened. The Complete Grip is the grip most favored by the author.

Another form of grip, and one which should be avoided at all costs, is the *Ice Pick Grip.* As in the case of the Hammer Grip, the Ice Pick Grip is a frequent choice of unskilled or deranged persons, and most particularly women, who in nine cases out of ten will instinctively use this grip.

The final form of grip to be discussed here is the type Applegate characterizes as the *Slash Attack Grip.* Another variant on this grip is the *Tjimande* style of holding the large *golok,* or cleaver knife, of the West Java area.

With the Slash Attack Grip, the knife is held with all fingers wrapped around the handle; the blade protruding from the little finger edge of the hand, palm down. In the *Tjimande* style, the blade is held in much the same fashion, except the palm is up, and the blade protrudes from the thumb edge of the hand. This is a rather poor form of grip, but nonetheless effective in the hands of a determined individual. Certain ethnic groups seem to have a particular affinity for this grip.

Loveless (at right) demonstrates the Slash Attack Grip.

Figure 47

Stance

Stance is perhaps the most important area of concern in the entire art of knife use. Incorrect stance is more than mere bad form — it is *deadly,* often leaving the knife wielder open to counter-thrusts, physical over-powering, and ultimately, death at the hands of a skilled enemy.

Correct stance is simple, easily learned, and should *never* be improvised upon. It is the result of a great deal of study, effort, and practical trial.

In the pages of this book, we refer to correct stance as *Battery Position:* a term borrowed from artillery nomenclature, which nevertheless manages to effectively portray what is meant by "correct."

Battery Position is as follows: the body is held erect, the chin is tucked slightly in, and the eyes are focused on the opponent. The right foot is extended in front of the body, and the knees are slightly bent in a semi-crouch. The knife is held in the right hand, with the Complete Grip (or grip of your choice); level at the waist. The pommel of the knife should almost touch the body, and the point of the knife should be in line with the cap of the right knee. The left hand is extended slightly forward, with the palm held toward the opponent. Care should be taken to avoid "telegraphing" moves with the shoulders.

The practice of holding the left palm facing the opponent may seem a bit unconventional to some, but rest assured there is a good reason. Assuming your opponent has a knife, and you instinctively attempt to block it (a totally incorrect move, but one we cannot rule out), you will probably be cut. If you are to be cut on the hand, it is preferable to be cut in the palm rather than the back of the hand. If you are cut in the palm, your "Extending Tendons" may be severed, but you will still be able to make a fist. If you are cut on the back of the hand, the "Flexing Tendons" may be severed, and the hand will be useless.

The best thing to remember is to avoid blocking with the hand, and thus avoid being cut. If you forget, and are cut, take steps to maximize your chances of retaliation. It's better to risk even a crippling injury than to risk death.

Various other forms of stance have been recommended, all of them having something, at least, in common with what we have here described as Battery Position; a few having minor differences. At the risk of making this book incomplete, the author has refrained from including them, for the simple reason that correct Battery Position cannot be improved upon. This may sound like a strong statement,

Figure 48

Correct Battery Position. Knife is pulled well into body, knees are slightly bent, left arm is barely extended, chin is tucked in and eyes are level.

Right profile of Battery Position. Chin could be tucked in a bit more.

Figure 49

Figure 50

Left profile of Battery Position. Knife hand is too far extended here, but notice how wrist is slightly cocked in preparation for cut.

and it's meant to be. The practice of knife fighting does not allow room for mistakes, and it is not the author's wish to cloud the reader's mind with useless, mistake-provoking information.

Thrusting

Thrusts from Battery Position should take the form of lightening-quick bursts of action. After each thrust, the knife should be snapped back into battery. While thrusting, take care not to fully commit the body's weight and momentum, but instead rely upon the strength of the arm and shoulder muscles. Avoid being drawn off balance during the thrust, as a skilled opponent may attempt to use your own force against you.

Use foot work to press against your opponent, rather than leaning into him. Attempt to move yourself in the manner of a fencer, allowing the right foot to, in essence, slide the left foot forward.

John Styers, in particular, has written an excellent exposition of the proper thrusting technique, and offers this bit of advice:

"On the thrust, the free arm has been whipped back, turning the full body with a snap. Instead of the full spread of the shoulders and chest which had been exposed to your opponent, you now present the narrowest view of your body. The upper portion on the body has pivoted forming a straight line from your blade point back along your arm, across the shoulders and down the free arm in the rear."

You will quickly notice that the thrust, when properly executed, does not cause you to shift the position of your right foot. The torque of the body's snap is taken up by the right knee, and the body trunk slightly lowered. When you practice this thrust, you will also find that it does not cause you to fully commit your body weight to an irretrievable movement. You can parry, press forward, or shift position easily.

Try this exercise: first, take up the Battery Position; second, effect a snap thrust, and while the arm is fully extended, take a slight "hop" forward with the right foot, allowing the left foot to slide along behind.

This exercise is an alternative to the *quick return* to Battery Position, and is beneficial in that it will help you to understand how it is possible to press forward against an opponent without sacrificing balance and mobility.

The quick return to Battery Postition does have its own benefits, as well. The quick return helps you to present a seemingly invincible front to your enemy, and constantly leaves you in a position from which to launch further attacks.

Figure 51

Preparing for the thrust. The body begins to twist.

Figure 52

The thrust in progress. Notice how the left arm is being thrown back, and how the left foot begins to travel.

Figure 53

Knife arms is extended, left arm is well back, body is still twisting and the left foot is still traveling.

Figure 54

The thrust complete. Although complete, however, notice how body's momentum is not irretrievably committed. Figures 51 through 54 were taken in a sequence-burst with a fully motorized camera at approximately three frames per second. This gives you an idea of the speed involved in a proper thrust.

Figure 55

Loveless (at right) times a thrust to opponent's head. From this position he can immediately effect an arm cut, or rapidly pull back. Were the opponents closer together, Loveless would throw more momentum into the thrust for a killing blow.

The quick return demands that you keep your body loose and limber; almost relaxed. The waist and hips are kept in fluid motion, while the arm and shoulders are tense with activity. Correct form is only gained afer considerable practice, but is well worth the added effort required.

When thrusting, is it proper to direct blows against specific targets? This is a question that may be on your mind, but unfortunately, there is no true pat answer. Frequently, it will be impossible to direct your thrusts to specific, carefully chosen target areas of your opponent's body. The reason for this is simple: any normal adult male, when faced with the probability of a knife fight, will be dealing with a natural amount of fear. Fear, unfortunately, leads to panic, and panic leads to a loss of discipline. Loss of discipline promotes blind thrusting to the main trunk area of the opponent's body.

How do we deal with this problem? Simply by making it work for us, rather than against us. *Controlled* loss of discipline (a contradiction in terms, but nevertheless valid), also has the tendency to create an almost unnatural speed, or agility. Because of this, the fighter well trained in the quick return thrust will be able to direct his attacks in a veritable barrage against his enemy. Instead of consciously picking and choosing targets; wasting valuable mental energy in the middle of a bad situation, the trained fighter will *act*, and act *fast*. His only thought will be the *thrust that hits*, rather than the thrust which may or may not reach its target.

Should thrusts be directed against specific targets? If there is a pat answer to this question, you may gather from the above that the answer could be "No." Remember that you are a human being, complete with all human emotions. Don't become obsessed with targets, and you won't become filled with blind fear and panic if you "miss" one. Concentrate on the *thrust that hits the body,* and keep thrusting until you master the conflict. When you are master of the conflict, only then can you afford the time it takes to direct the final, killing blow.

Slashing

A slash with the knife may be thought of as an adjunct to the tactic of thrusting. Often, a thrust that is harmless can turn into a slash that acts with telling effect.

Cutting and slashing are the tactics most often used in the preliminary moments of a knife fight. They are frequently directed against the face, arms, hands, legs or throat of the enemy. While it is difficult to slash a man to death, a steady barage of such blows will have the effect of destroying the enemy's ability to retaliate, and allow the figher time to direct his final blow.

Cuts and slashes are of two kinds: vertical and horizontal. To be sure, it is also possible to direct diagonal slashes, but these will, in the main, be employed against the chest and stomach of the enemy, and are better avoided. With the vertical slashes your aim is to sever vital tendons and blood vessels of the arm, wrist, hand or shoulders. With horizontal slashes you concern yourself against the face, throat, or legs of your enemy.

When executing the slash or cut, try to cock your hand slightly backward at the wrist, and allow the force of the falling blade to provide momentum. Avoid assisting this natural momentum with the wrist.

Try this exercise: first, cock the hand; next, snap it forward, and at the same time, when the blade is in line with the arm, lock the hand, wrist and forearm into a mass of tension. Train yourself to

The Hand Cut (or Vertical Cut) in progress. Notice how Loveless (at right) has wrist slightly cocked just before contact.

place the greatest tension and control in the forearm and wrist, gradually relaxing your arm in the area between elbow and shoulder.

This practice of tensing the forearm and wrist while relaxing the elbow, biceps and shoulder was taught to the author by an Asian instructor who used the following reasoning to back up his argument:

"When the arm is tense along its entire length, it is like the limb of a tree. It does not bend when assailed, it only breaks."

What is meant here is that the slash should not place the fighter in an untenable position; one in which a trained opponent could use the stiffly extended arm as a means to throw, or disarm him. It will also be discovered that the method here recommended will allow the spring of the slashing blade to be controlled from the elbow, rather than the wrist, adding greater power to the movement.

A common defense against the extended arm is to break it at the elbow. Should your opponent be aware of this defense, and attempt to parry your slash, he will find himself quite surprised when you again cock your hand and again slash or chop at him. This is particularly important when executing a horizontal slash. If you miss, or if the opponent dodges, he can move against your extended arm, using your own momentum against you, and break your arm over his knee.

Unlike the thrust, the slash is better directed against a target. The target in this case is rather loosely defined, however, being the area of your opponent's body which happens to be most accessible to you: his arms and hands.

The key here is to remember our previous statements, back in Part I; the statements which counseled you to inflict maximum damage when you are inside your enemy's field of action. The slash or cut (and, indeed, the thrust), will place you well inside this field of action. Thus, if you miss with a slash to your enemy's left hand, it will be best if your slash was aimed in such a manner as will allow you to carry your movement over to his right hand.

The message here is simple: don't "aim" for just one target, "aim" for two, three, four, or as many as you can hit. *Never* commit yourself to a single area of your opponent's body. *Always* make every single action do double duty.

Arms and hands make the best targets for slashing, for the simple reason there are two of them. You need not panic or lose your composure if a slash to one is ineffectual, as you'll usually have a second chance. *Anything* that gets in the way of your knife during a slash is going to be cut. If your hand, wrist and forearm are properly

Detail of hand cut. Notice how forearm is tense while bicep is relaxed.

Figure 57

held, and the knife cocked before each slash, the cut is going to be deep and damaging. You'll be well on your way to leaving the contest alive.

Mental Discipline

A while back we mentioned something called "controlled loss of discipline." We also mentioned that this might be a contradiction in terms, but is nevertheless a valid phenomena.

What we're doing here is creating discipline on the foundations of an undisciplined situation: a fight or conflict in which life is at stake. We're accepting the fact that normal men are going to have to deal with normal emotions: emotions like fear, rage, blind anger, panic or hysteria. If you think you might be different, you're only kidding yourself. Men with experience in actual close quarter combat situations will readily attest that it's no joke when death stares you in the face, or when men are dying around you.

The natural reaction of most individuals to negative emotions is to attempt to control these emotions by force, or will-power. The tendency is to cut off negative emotions; to bottle them up, or deny they exist. Indeed, this is the tactic employed in most training programs: negative emotions and emotional reactions are "covered

Horizontal slash directed to the arm.

Figure

Figure 59

Horizontal slash to arm is immediately followed by horizontal slash to throat. Notice how Loveless keeps well away from Randall's blade.

up'' by alledgedly instilling the trainee with confidence. This confidence is supposed to come from a sound knowledge of the tactics, and the experience that comes from training.

While this method has a great deal to recommend itself, it isn't foolproof, as a glance at casualty lists will tell us. It's a particularly poor tactic when the trainee is faced with the prospect of a fanatical enemy; one who is pumped up on ideals, drugs, or a combination of both. We're living in an era where old rules of combat no longer apply. Today, particularly in areas where guerilla activity is prevalent, we have to realize that the opponent we face may care little for his own life.

So what do we do when we're faced with an enemy on a suicide mission? Does all our training and confidence fly out the window? The answer to these questions is not a simple one, as the over-all question is one which only a few training programs are now coming to grips with. This is an area of comparitively recent thought; principally confined to the tactic of counter-ambush.

For the purposes of this book, we're going to examine a method of mental discipline which attempts to *use* negative emotions, rather than cover them up. We're not talking about counter-ambush *per se*

91

Figure 60

Another sequence-burst with the motorized camera, illustrating the slash, here beginning.

Figure 61

The slash in mid-position.

Figure 62

The slash at peak of movement.

— which is really only another exercise in confidence-building and saturation training. Instead we're talking about the *transformation* of negatives into strengths.

Part of what we're talking about may be better understood by re-reading the comments regarding the tactic of thrusting. There, instead of becoming obsessed with fear, we learned of possible advantages, i.e. the tendency for the normal human to act with haste in a fearful situation. Of course training played its part, and with that training came a certain amount of new confidence.

Beyond that, however, we may begin to realize that it is possible not to be *afraid of fear*. Instead of denying the existence of fear and becoming rigid, we can learn to accept its presence and thus become flexible. If we are faced with a fanatical opponent, or if we are taken by surprise, we're not overwhelmed by the appearance of our own emotional response. Instead we *act*.

Fear is by no means the only emotion the knife figher has to deal with. The other, possibly more difficult emotion is anger or rage. As in the case of fear, rage has the quality of promoting blind action. A man caught by anger doesn't use his mind, he only uses his body. His senses are dulled by the intensity of his feelings, and he becomes an easy mark for the skilled opponent.

In order to help us deal with anger, it will be beneficial to divide it into two categories —
   1. "Hot" anger;
   2. "Cold" anger.

Briefly, we will characterize the first category as the type of anger which causes a man to lose control of himself. The second category we will characterize as something which helps the fighter dominate the conflict.

Our goal here is to transform "hot" anger into "cold" anger. We can achieve this goal by realizing and appreciating the *power* of anger as a means for focusing energy.

Assume for a moment you are a party to a knife fight. You opponent cuts you, you become enraged at him, and seek to kill him quickly. Your anger builds, you rush at your opponent and in your fury knock him down, falling upon him with your knife. It does not matter to you that he is armed, or that you may again be injured by him. You seek only to kill him by any means, no matter the cost to yourself.

To carry our assumptions a bit further, we will suppose that your opponent is indeed well armed, and when you fall upon him you fall upon his knife, thus dealing yourself a killing blow. In your rage you did not think of this possibility, or if you did, you didn't care. This is,

Figure 63

Transform negative emotions into tactic. Do anything to keep your own mind clear, and don't worry about how you might or might not appear. The fighter here grits his teeth and turns anger into action.

perhaps, an extreme example, but it serves to illustrate what is meant by "hot" anger: the careless spending of energy.

To illustrate how this "hot" anger may be transformed, let us now suppose another knife fight: again, you are angry at your opponent, but this time instead of allowing the anger to control you, you control it.

You transform anger into tactic, and that is the key. Each snap thrust directed to your enemy is filled with anger, and you visualize the anger flowing through your arms into your knife. You allow emotion to show in your face, and present your enemy with a fearsome spectacle. You attempt to convince youself that the anger you may feel is being manifested in your carefully learned tactics of grip, stance, thrust and slash. Anger is no longer an emotion. It is, instead, an *activity.* It is not blind activity, but a skilled activity: knife fighting — something in which you are trained, and clearly understand.

Lest the reader believe that these remarks are the result of the author's idle musings, or that this course of study is unimportant, it would be well to point out that what we are here discussing is a practice which dates back thousands of years, and forms the nucleus of many of the world's great combat systems. If there is any "secret" to Asia's fighting styles, this is it: mental discipline.

Mental discipline and the study of emotion is not mumbo-jumbo. It is what separates men from animals, and is the deciding factor between the novice knife fighter and the master. Understand this well: in a knife fight you are seeking to control your opponent in order to defeat him. To do this, you must learn to control yourself. To put it another way: if you don't control yourself, you may find that your enemy will do it for you.

The reader who is interested in furthering his studies along these lines is advised to obtain a copy of *Asian Fighting Arts,* by Donn. F. Draeger and Robert W. Smith (New York: Berkeley Publishing Corporation, 1974). This book is an excellent introduction to the various martial disciplines of the East, and provides much valuable commentary on the subject of mental discipline and the fighting man.

TACTICAL MOVEMENT

With the basics of knife fighting behind us, we may again continue with our study of specific tactics. To do this properly, we must first learn to distinguish between *movement* and *maneuver.*

Movement is the exertion of physical and mental energy. Maneuver is made up of *tactical movement:* movement according to plan, with a definite goal in mind. Knife fighting is tactical movement, but we must not learn to think of it in terms of pure maneuver. Although we do have a goal (to kill our enemy), we cannot proceed to this goal by means of an orderly plan. Knife fighting is not the same as fencing. It is not a formal, structured situation into which set maneuvers may be introduced. Thus, we concentrate upon refining action. We learn a number of specific tactical movements, which we string together according to the demands of each encounter.

Earlier, we advanced the theory that all offensive and defensive actions are basically the same thing. Accordingly, we will examine tactical movement in this context.

Gripping your knife correctly, standing correctly, thrusting and slashing correctly are all tactical movements of a primary order. They are the foundation upon which the fight is built. It is upon this foundation that we begin:

We begin with the absence of any preconceived notions about our adversary; a willingness to accept any movement on his part without letting it affect our original intention, and the absence of a planned "first strike." Momentary stillness is to be favored over immediate aggression.

The active opponent is the easiest to kill. His mind is made up, his course of action decided upon, and he usually has only brute strength

Figure 64

Loveless (at right) feints low to draw Randall.

Loveless times slash to Randall's throat and face while springing from feint.

Figure 65

Figure 66

The fighter following a low feint or pulled slash puts his head and arm well within your reach.

and force to accomplish his aims. *Your first tactic is to wait for him to move, or to goad him into movement by means of the feint.*

He may be running at you, screaming at the top of his lungs, waving his blade wildly, or he may be silently creeping toward you, his blade firmly in hand and a set look in his eyes. In either case, his movement indicates mental activity, i.e., a "decision" or commitment to a course of action. Speed of his movement is of little relevance, but your replying tactic is essential. He is attacking you and he expects you to attempt evasion. If at all possible, do *not* evade him. Instead, strike for the opening his movement has created. This then is your second tactic: *counter-attack.*

Remember — a man cannot harm you if —

1. He doesn't know your next move;
2. He has the wrong "information" about your next move;
3. He has a preconceived notion about your next move;
4. He is firmly and blindly commited to his own move.

We have before us two tactics: the feint and the counter-attack. How do we execute these movements? Simply by building upon the tactical movements of correct grip, correct stance, the thrust and the slash. We feint from correct stance with our knee or shoulder, knife hand or free hand. Feinting movement to the right, our attacker thrusts to the right. We strike him with a thrust or slash to his unprotected left. If our attacker is already in motion, committed to a certain course of action, we do not feint. Instead, we *remain motionless until he reaches the perimeter of our effective field of action.* Then we employ the thrust or slash with telling effect.

At no time do we allow the adversary to enter our effective field of action unassailed. This is our third tactic: *a defined area of movement.* At all times when the adversary is within our field of action *we are on the offensive!* It is a case of the best defense being a strong offense.

Our fourth tactic is as follows: *when the adversary leaves our field of action, we immediately return to battery.* In many cases, this will have the effect of drawing him into pressing his attack. If it does not, and only if our opponent is sufficiently weakened, we employ our fifth tactic: *we enter his field of action.* This entry should, ideally, be introduced by the tactic of feinting, followed by a combination of slashes. Thrusts should be with-held until the concluding moments of the fight. The purpose of withdrawing to battery is easily explained: by doing so, you are always in a position to deal with any further activity on the part of your adversary, and are well-prepared to make your counter-moves.

Let's pause for a moment, reflect upon these tactics, and then go on to a few random observations regarding actual combat.

Figure 67

Loveless (at right) illustrates the beginning of all tactics the Battery Position. Here, he senses that Randall is about to throw a thrust, and is within his field of action.

Loveless executes *Passata Sotto* in response to Randall's thrust.

Figure 68

Figure 69

Following *Passata Sotto* Battery Position is immediately regained. Figures 67 through 69 illustrate how defense and offense are virtually the same.

The five building blocks of tactical movement are —
1. Correct Grip;
2. Battery Position;
3. Snap Thrusts;
4. Multiple Slashes;
5. Mental Discipline.

The tactical movements to learn and practice are —
1. Wait for an opening (Let your enemy move first);
2. Feint to create an opening (Make him move);
3. Counter-attack (Cut and thrust);
4. Move within a defined area (Learn your effective field of action);
5. Return to Battery Position (When enemy leaves your field of action);
6. Take the offense (When enemy is weakened, attack with slashes);
7. Kill with the thrust.

Random Observations

Perhaps the most glaring fault of modern knife fighting instruction — and this applies to many systems — is that it presupposes the opponent to possess the same psychology as the trainee.

This can be fatal. There are no "absolutes" in knife fighting. When any tactic other than the Sneak Attack is brought into play, knife fighting becomes equally lethal to both parties involved. Avoid pre-conceived notions about your opponent, save one: always imagine he is better than you.

Physically slight men often have the advantage over those of more impressive build. This is largely due to the small man being frequently underestimated by his opponent; the small man's ability to move rapidly, and his knowledge of his own inequality of physique. Although it is often sheer suicide to make general statements about potential adversaries, I will risk here the judgement that larger men, even while engaged in quick movements, have a unique tendency to —

1. Leave substantial openings in their defense;
2. Bring both hands into action.

A larger man's ego is often his own worst enemy. A smaller man's awareness of his own deficiencies is often his strongest defense.

By this I do not mean to say that the smaller man should experience other than normal caution at the sight of a formidable opponent. Quite the contrary. The smaller individual should cultivate an attitude of satisfaction at the sight of a large adversary, if only for the simple reason that there is so much more to strike against. We are not talking about brute strength here; we're talking about guts, speed, and brain power.

A physically large man's best defense is to resist the impulse to "crush" an opponent. Leave bear-like grappling holds, "hugs" and strikes to the bears. Use brain instead of muscle, and the chances are you'll come out of your encounter alive.

Speech is very deadly. When engaging an opponent *keep your mouth shut!* Do not attempt to inspire fear, caution, or create subterfuge by words. Seek only to inflict maximum physical damage. The very act of speaking presupposes mental activity, and wastes precious mental energy and awareness. Remember that actions speak louder than words.

Here's an observation you may find surprising: women are among the most dangerous adversaries a knife fighter may face. Because women are generally thought of as the ''weaker sex'' a man will be less inclined to use maximum force or tactical advantage. Women are, as a rule, more prone to use the knife as an offensive weapon, frequently without warning. Most women are also capable of greater emotional focus than men. This may take the form of blind rage or cold-blooded cunning, and both are equally dangerous. In Asia, some parts of the Middle East and in Latin America, women have been skilled in the use of the knife for generations and are proud of this fact. Behave as a gentleman would when dealing with ladies, but remember that the female with knife in hand can be deadlier than the male.

STYLE AND MANEUVER

We come now to an examination of the various commentaries and recommendations put forth by Fairbairn, Biddle, Applegate and Styers — in a strictly practical sense. We'll be looking at the specific tactics of these gentlemen, impartially, and the reader is advised to draw his own conclusions as to the merits of each.

We separate the techniques of these gentlemen from the techniques outlined in the previous chapter by refering to them as "maneuver." Why? You will remember that we defined maneuver as "tactical movement: movement according to plan." As you will readily see, the following methods are complete within themselves, and thus fall into the category of maneuver rather than pure tactical movement. In many cases, these maneuvers are built of two or more moves.

A Comparison of Form

In certain instances, the difference between a given maneuver advocated by one instructor and that of another, is only a matter of style, or form. To examine the subtle nuances of each, by way of comparison, actually serves no good purpose. If we are to make any comparison of these forms, it would be much more beneficial to compare them in terms of maximum advantages gained by their execution, i.e., which particular maneuver is "best" or most effective? Which maneuver will we add to our arsenal of tactics?

As grip, stance, thrusting and slashing have been treated separately, we will here examine only that which is left to us: the remaining tactics or maneuvers of attack and defense.

Elsewhere in this book we have mentioned the terms *In-quartata, Stoccata,* and *Passata Sotto.* These are terms from fencing which have been adopted by Western instructors to refer to knife fighting maneuvers which combine the elements of feint and attack, or thrust. Biddle and Styers are the two most notable proponents of these maneuvers.

In-quartata is accomplished by executing a full thrust-type movement, at the same time throwing the rear, or left leg to the rear and right of the right foot, which is used as a pivotal point. It is done in response to a thrust by your enemy, placing you at an angle to him, and thus safe from his thrust. At the point when you are executing *In-quartata,* it is recommended that you use your knife to effect either a hand-cut or a full thrust to the head or throat.

This movement is essentially a dodge, which allows your enemy's blade to pass by you harmlessly, followed by an offensive action, such

Figure 70

In-Quartata. Loveless (at right) perfectly illustrates the form of this move recommended by Biddle.

This photo was not posed. It was taken during the course of action at a fencing tournament. The fencer at left is beginning to execute *In-Quartata.* Notice how his left foot is well up and off the ground, traveling to the rear and right of his right foot. As this fencer's movement progressed, his left arm was thrown well back. Notice also how his opponent's sword is at this point harmlessly by-passed.

Figure 71

Figure 72

Stocatta, in the style of Biddle.

Right view of Stocatta, showing how the adversary's blade is avoided.

Figure 73

as the thrust or cut. It is stated that your enemy's momentum will probably cause him to be carried to, or past, your original position, and thus it will be difficult for him to dodge your blade. He will be well within arm's length, and a prime target. In practicing *In-quartata* it might be well for you to observe whether or not you are firmly grounded and balanced, with the left foot to the right of the right foot. It will help if you keep your knees slightly bent during this maneuver, as with the feet in this position, a strong enemy may be able to topple you to the side, or cause you to become tangled by your own legs.

Stoccata is merely the opposite of *In-quartata,* although it does not require as much of an unnatural foot position. It is used when your enemy directs a high, wheeling thrust to your head — slightly turning his body — presenting a portion of his back to you.

Again using your right foot as a pivotal point, instead of crossing your left foot behind, you throw it well in front of your right foot — keeping your body at an angle — and direct a thrust to your enemy's side or kidney. It is best if you accompany this thrust by throwing your free arm slightly over your head. From this position, you may be able to launch a ''chop'' or blow against your enemy's neck.

Another form of *Stoccata* is where you throw your left foot to the left, in a line with your right foot, rather than in front of it. From this position you strike to your enemy's mid-section. Your free arm is thrown to the rear, as with *In-quartata,* and your body turned at the waist to present less of a target to your enemy. It should be noted that both forms of *Stoccata* are accompanied by a rapid lowering of the body by bending at the knees.

The second form of *Stoccata* presented above is the type thought to be the most beneficial. As you will learn from practice, this move allows you to keep your balance at all times, as both feet are firmly planted and a certain ''spring'' is retained in the legs. It is recommended that you learn and study both forms, practicing them until you are proficient. With many opponents, they will be found to be quite beneficial. A trained knife fighter, on the other hand, may be prepared for such manuevers, and may not allow himself to be drawn into executing wild thrusts.

Passata Sotto is another response to the high thrust, as well as a means to bring your enemy's head into range for the horizontal slash or a thrust.

With this maneuver, you suddenly drop your torso extremely low and to the left of Battery Position. It has been recommended that the left hand be placed upon the ground to steady the body, or alternatively, that the left arm be thrown back on a line with the left leg.

Figure 74

Again, this photo was not posed. It was taken in the heat of an Olympic try-out. The fencer at right is captured in the middle of executing *Stocatta*. Although his form is adequate for fencing purposes, his left foot is a bit too far backward for modern knife fighting. The instant after this photograph was taken, however, the fencer's strategy became apparent. His was a "false" *Stocatta*, which allowed him to slip into a beautifully executed *Passata Sotto*. He scored his point and won the match.

In *Passata Sotto*, the left knee should almost touch the ground, but never should it be allowed to come to rest.

When executed against a thrust, your counter-thrust should be timed to reach the enemy's lower right chest, stomach, or groin. If your enemy follows your sudden dip, attempt a horizontal slash to the head. He will, in all probability, be in a somewhat guarded position when reacting to your *Passata Sotto*, so care must be taken to avoid his counter-tactic.

Figure 75

Full *Passata Sotto*. The left knee does not touch the ground, and the fighter may immediately spring back.

Outside parry and grab, according to Biddle.

Figure 76

Figure 77

Inside parry and grab (after Biddle), here illustrated with a quick thrust to the opponent's throat.

Rex Applegate's famous back-hand assassin's trick. Knife is thrust backwards into victim's kidney as assassin strides past.

Figure 78

Randall throws the dust to distract his opponent, and at the same time draws his blade.

Figure 80

Figure 79

Figure 81

Randall immediately gains Battery Position, and begins to launch attack.

Ray Randall here illustrates the method of drawing a boot knife. He crouches for the draw, and at the same time reaches for a handful of dust or dirt.

Figure 82

Use of the stick in "Object" Defense. Ray Randall holds the stick in guard position recommended by Fairbairn.

An excellent variation on *Passata Sotto* is to rapidly "bob up and down." Execute the maneuver to draw your opponent to a low, or crouching position, then spring back to your original height. When making this spring, simultaneously execute a horizontal slash to his face, and pull back rapidly. The simultaneous slash, spring and pull back will help guard against a thrust being directed toward your abdomen. When practicing *Passata Sotto,* become conscious of the possibility of being over-powered while in a low position. It is well to extend your knife arm to discouarge kicks and make thrusts, but take care not to fall into the habit of allowing it to remain fully extended for long periods. Your arm will be quite vulnerable in this position, as it is somewhat difficult to return to Battery Position quickly while executing *Passata Sotto.*

DEFENSE

We come now to the final area of maneuver to be considered in this book: *defense.* Actually, the study of defense against the knife is better confined to books covering the martial arts of *karate-do, silat, wu shu, aiki-do* or others, rather than books treating the field of knife fighting. The reason is a simple one: the best defense against the knife is a strong offense with the knife (or gun, or club, or chain, etcetera). The man or woman who contemplates facing the knife while unarmed would do well to run. If running isn't in your nature, or is impossible, and if you do not choose to go armed yourself, then

Figure 83

Randall times a butt-stroke to his opponent's head.

by all means take up the study of one of the martial arts listed above. *Silat,* the Indonesian art, is a particularly effective system for unarmed defense against the knife; perhaps the best yet devised. This is because Indonesia, unlike many other areas, has a strong tradition of small-blade k-.ife fighting (in versus of sword fighting). It is only natural then, that *Silat* would have developed excellent counter-knife measures.

The reader interested in furthering his research along these lines, as well as the reader who is interested in all forms of martial culture, weaponry, and tactic is strongly advised to obtain a subscription to *Martial Arts International.* M.A.I. is, without question, the best magazine ever published in this field. Subscriptions are U.S. $10.00 per year, and may be purchased by writing to M.A.I. at P.O. Box 1241, Kealakekua, Hawaii 96750. Malaysian readers should forward their subscription orders to M.A.I. at P.O. Box 550, Penang, Malaysia. As this magazine is produced in Asia by recognized authorities, the reader is assured of receiving accurate, responsible information and advice. Thus, *Martial Arts International* is an indispensable addition to every serious knife fighter's library.

To return to our discussion of defense: as virtually all previous books on the subject of knife fighting have included chapters on unarmed defense against the knife, the author has decided not to "break step," and here includes a digest of the various methods employed.

Figure 84

Randall's left hand is sliding down the stick as he immediately pulls back following the butt-stroke,

Applegate, who has done the greatest amount of work along these lines, has delineated four basic forms of defense —

1. "Object" defense (chairs, sticks, etcetera);
2. Knee kicks;
3. Parry;
4. Block.

These four methods will, by and large, be suitable for dealing with most situations. Although various other forms of knife defense have been advocated by different instructors, their methods will, in the main, be based upon these same four categories.

The use of an *object* as a means of defense is well established. To many, the proper response to a knife attack is a coat artfully wrapped about the arm. This is a technique acquired from motion pictures and television, and a virtual waste of time. The more proper method of using an article of clothing for defense copies the bull-fighter, or *matador*. Instead of wrapping the coat about the arm, the defender seeks to entangle the attacker's blade, throw the coat in his eyes, or make some similar maneuver. These last techniques have their basis in 17th and 18th century rapier play, and owe their greater origins to the mesh net used by Roman gladiators.

In close, urban quarters where a coat is not available, a chair is recommended. The defender in this case uses his chair in the manner of the circus lion-tamer; seeking to tangle the attacker's arms and hands in the chair's legs.

Figure 85

Now well away from his opponent, Randall executes a downward strike to the collarbone. This is a particularly effective method of using the stick.

If a chair is not available, *anything* which comes to hand may be of value, the primary object being to prevent the attacker from effectively using his knife. When this has been accomplished, the defender proceeds to belabour the attacker with fists and feet, at all times remaining wary of the blade.

In addition to coats, chairs, or any large objects, the use of dust and dirt is also advocated. The defender stoops quickly, grabs a handful of dirt and throws it into the attacker's eyes. This is followed by either a hasty retreat, or a series of blows, depending entirely upon the nature of the situation.

The military man's helmet also makes an effective defense object only in this case it should be used as a small shield rather than a projectile. Throwing your helmet at your attacker leaves you empty handed. Grasping your helmet by the liner or webbing and using it as a parrying shield at least gives you a fighting chance.

The final object to be mentioned here is the stick, or cane. The stick is, perhaps, the best method of dealing with a knife when a gun, chain, or other knife is not available. Stick or staff fighting is, indeed, an art unto itself, and well-timed blows with the stick are capable of inflicting serious injury and death. Against the knife, the stick is first used to parry the attacker's thrust, and then to deliver a blow to his temple, nose or jaw. These blows are followed by chopping stabs and punches to the throat — using the end of the stick — and the attacker is finished off by kicks or strangulation.

Figure 86

Kicks to the knee should place the defender well away from the opponent's blade.

Kicks to the groin area need not be described to be appreciated.

Figure 87

Figure 88

Always parry with the forearm.

Do not try to parry or block with the hand! A strong opponent may "tear" past your thumb.

Figure 89

Figure 90

Although it is well to block with both arms, the block shown here is not completely correct. The attacker is already well into his downward thrust. This thrust should have been blocked *before* it gained momentum.

Again, with all forms of object defense, the idea is to first thwart or disarm the attacker, and only then to finish him off with kicks or blows. As each situation tends to breed its own rules, further generalizations are not practically possible.

Knee kicks are the second form of defense to be considered. Also included here are all forms of foot-work, whether directed against the knee, instep, groin or other targets. The object in using the feet is to —

1. Throw the trunk of the body out of range,
2. Kick the attacker off balance, keeping him away.

A well-timed forceful kick will frequently be enough to down an attacker of average build, or at least give him pause. Take the advantage this pause provides to stamp on the knife hand, kick him in the ribs or in the head, or attempt to gouge his eyes. Sharply delivered blows with the point of the toe are best directed to the base of the spine, or to the groin. Both can disable even the strongest attacker.

The third form of defense, that of the *parry,* is best effected by using the forearm; the hand being balled into a fist. The parry may be used against downward thrusts; upward thrusts, and both right or left hand slashes, when directed from the ''outside'' in a wheeling, or circular motion.

You may use either the inside of your forearm or the outside, depending upon the demands of the situation. The object is, first and foremost, to divert your opponent's thrust harmlessly away from your body.

Using the inside of your forearm, you hook the attacker's knife arm — pushing it backwards — and at the same time knee him in the groin. With your left, or free hand, you firmly grasp his wrist — pushing the blade even further away from you — and attempt to break the attacker's arm at the elbow or dislocate his shoulder. It is also possible to break or sprain his wrist.

Although there are methods where the left hand is used to parry or grab the attacker's knife arm, they are fraught with danger and better avoided. A good, general rule is to always parry with the same arm as the attacker's knife arm. Thus, if your attacker is right handed, parry with your right arm instead of grabbing with your left.

The final method to be discussed is the *block.* The first general rule is to always time your block to contact the attacker's arm *before his thrust commences.* The second general rule is to *avoid the use of the hand,* and the third rule is to always follow every block with *immediate offensive action.*

The block is best used against the downward thrust, and, as in the case of parrying, the forearm is the recommended portion of your anatomy to be used. The hand is to be avoided for the simple reason that a formidable enemy may be able to push past your thumb with the momentum of this thrust.

It is for this same reason that you attempt to block your attacker before he builds up momentum. Upon blocking his arm, waste no time in following with a knee or kick to the groin, and you will be able to quell whatever force he may still possess.

Blocks may also be followed by foot throws or arm locks. When effecting a block with the right arm, reach well into your attacker with the left arm and hand; directing a chop to his throat. Slide your blocking arm to the point where you can grasp his wrist with your right hand, and while keeping your left arm locked over the attacker's right shoulder — in front of his throat — place your left leg behind his right knee; throwing him backwards.

As with the three other basic forms of defense we have discussed, the block lends itself well to experimentation and practice. Continual training in these defenses will assist the knife fighter should he become accidentally disarmed. They are also useful for developing expertise with the left, or free arm. It must be stressed, however, that defense against the knife forms a study apart from the study of knife fighting. It is well to know how to parry and block with coat, chair, arm or hand, but the truly effective fighter must also know how to finish the contest with further movements. It is for these movements that we must return to the martial arts.

Bibliography

Agrippa, Camillo. *Trattato di Scienza d'Arme.* Venice, 1604.

Applegate, Rex (Lieutenant Colonel). *Kill or Get Killed.* Fourth Edition. Harrisburg: The Stackpole Company, 1969.

Applegate, Rex. *Crowd and Riot Control.* Harrisburg: The Stackpole Company, 1969.

Biddle, A.J.D. (Lieutenant Colonel). *Do or Die: A Supplementary Manual on Individual Combat.* 1937. Reprint. Boulder: Paladin Press, 1974.

Cassidy, William L., ed. *Knife Digest.* First Edition. Berkeley: Knife Digest Publishing Company, Inc., 1974.

Cassidy, William L. "Every Gambler Needs One: An Inquisitive Essay Regarding the Push Dirk." *American Blade,* January-February 1974, pp. 30-35.

Cassidy, William L. *The Fighting Knife in Modern Warfare: Notes on the Design and Specification of the Tactical-Survivor Fighting Knife.* Unpublished document for use of contractor and manufacturing engineers. (Restricted) Berkeley, 1975.

Cassidy, William. *Switchblades and Special Edged Weapons: Their Development and Use.* Forthcoming.

Castle, Egerton. *Schools and Masters of Fence, From the Middle Ages to the End of the Eighteenth Century.* London: George Bell & Sons, 1892.

d'Avillier, Charles and Dore, Gustave. *The Navaja and its Use in Spain.* London, 1881.

Draeger, Donn F. *Weapons & Fighting Arts of the Indonesian Archipelago.* Rutland and Tokyo: Charles E. Tuttle Company, 1972.

Draeger, Donn F. *Classic Bujutsu, The Martial Arts and Ways of Japan: Volume I.* New York and Tokyo: Weatherhill, 1973.

Draeger, Donn F. and Smith, Robert W. *Asian Fighting Arts.* New York: Berkeley Publishing Corporation, 1974.

Ek, John and Ek, Robert. *Your Silent Partner: A Handbook on Knife Fighting.* Nineteenth Edition. Miami, 1971.

Fairbairn, W.E. (Major). *Get Tough! How to Win in Hand-to-Hand Fighting.* New York and London: D. Appleton-Century Company, 1942.

Fairbairn, W.E. (Major). *All-In Fighting.* London: Faber & Faber, Ltd., 1941.

King-Harman, M.J. (Colonel). "Sword and Pistol." *Journal of the Military Service Institution,* January, 1897, pp. 115-126.

Loveless, Robert W., ed. *The Knifemakers Guild Directory of the Membership.* Riverside: Guild Publishers, 1974.

Manual del Baratero o Arte de Manejar la Navaja el Cuchillo y la Tijera de los Jitanos. Madrid, 1849.

Page, Camille. *La Coutellerie depuis l'origine jusqu'a nos jours, fabrication ancienne et moderne.* Six volumes. Paris: Chatellerault, impr. de H. Riviere, 1896-1904.

Peterson, Harold L. *American Knives: The First History and Collectors' Guide.* New York: Charles Scribner's Sons, 1958.

Peterson, Harold L. *Daggers & Fighting Knives of the Western World: From the Stone Age till 1900.* New York: Walker & Company, 1968.

Pitkin, Thomas M. "Quartermaster Equipment for Special Forces." *Q.M.C. Historical Studies.* Number Five. Washington, 1944.

Randall, Jr., W.D. and Applegate, Rex. *The Fighting Knife.* Fifteenth Edition. Orlando, 1969.

Styers, John and Schuon, Karl. *Cold Steel.* 1959. Reprint. Boulder: Paladin Press, 1974.

Truman, Ben C. (Major). *The Field of Honor: A Complete and Comprehensive History of Duelling in All Countries.* New York: Fords, Howard & Hulbert, 1884.

Wagner, Eduard. *Cut and Thrust Weapons.* New York: Spring Books, 1969.

Wise, Arthur. *The Art and History of Personal Combat.* New York: New York Graphic Soceity, Ltd., 1972.

Periodicals

American Blade. William L. Cassidy, editor. New Orleans: Southern House Publications, Inc.

Martial Arts International. Quinton T.G. Chambers, editor. Kealakekua, Hawaii: Martial Arts International.

Military Documents

War Department. 1942. *Unarmed Defense for the American Soldier.* Basic Field Manual FM 21-150. Washington.

Department of the Army. 1954. *Hand-to-Hand Combat.* Department of the Army Field Manual FM 21-150. Washington.

Department of the Army. 1953. *Bayonet.* Department of the Army Field Manual FM 23-25 (Restricted). Washington.

Navy Department. 1950. *Landing Party Manual, 1950, United States Navy.* Washington.